Introduction to
MUSHROOM HUNTING

VERA K. CHARLES

Formerly Associate Pathologist,
Office of Mycology and Disease Survey,
Bureau of Plant Industry

DOVER PUBLICATIONS, INC.
NEW YORK

CONTENTS

	Page		Page
Introduction	1	Phallaceae (stinkhorn fungi)	52
Danger from poisonous fungi	3	Lycoperdaceae (puffballs)	53
Agaricaceae (gill fungi)	4	Ascomycetes (sac fungi)	56
Polyporaceae (pore fungi)	43	Collateral reading	58
Hydnaceae (tooth fungi)	51	Glossary	59
Clavariaceae (coral fungi)	51	Index of species	60

Published in Canada by General Publishing Company, Ltd., 30 Lesmill Road, Don Mills, Toronto, Ontario.

Published in the United Kingdom by Constable and Company, Ltd., 10 Orange Street, London WC 2.

This Dover edition, first published in 1974, is an unabridged republication of the U. S. Department of Agriculture Circular No. 143, originally titled *Some Common Mushrooms and How to Know Them*. The work was first issued by the U. S. Government Printing Office in March, 1931, and slightly revised in August, 1946.

International Standard Book Number: 0-486-20667-X
Library of Congress Catalog Card Number: 73-85355

Manufactured in the United States of America
Dover Publications, Inc.
180 Varick Street
New York, N. Y. 10014

Introduction

A study of the wild mushrooms of the fields and woods makes its appeal to the amateur collector and the lover of nature as well as to the scientist. The beautiful colors and delicate textures exhibited by many of these plants offer a great attraction to the artistic, while the more practical are reminded of the gastronomic possibilities [2] offered by many of the wild species. To the more advanced student, the great variety in form and the detailed microscopic characters provide an unlimited field for investigation. The hope of finding something new continually urges one on, and the thrill of possible discovery is ever present.

The principal object of this circular is to provide the amateur collector or nature student with a convenient, safe, and practical means for the determination of some of the more common mushrooms and certain other interesting or conspicuous forms of fungi. It is hoped and confidently believed that an acquaintance with these humble dwellers of the woods and fields will add a real and vital interest to a walk or a day spent in the open.

In order that this circular may be of service to the largest number of people, species of common occurrence and wide geographic range have been selected for discussion.

---

[1] In this circular the term "mushroom" is not restricted to the Agaricaceae (gill fungi), but is used in a general sense to cover the larger fungi, in accordance with popular usage. This circular is in part a revision of and supersedes United States Department of Agriculture Bulletin 175, Mushrooms and Other Common Fungi, and Farmers' Bulletin 796, Some Common Edible and Poisonous Mushrooms.

[2] Requests for information about cooking mushrooms should be addressed to the Bureau of Home Economics, U. S. Department of Agriculture.

FUNGI IN GENERAL

The plants known as fungi comprise a very large group and exhibit great variation in form, size, color, and habit. The one important character common to all fungi is the absence of the green coloring matter known as chlorophyll, by means of which, through the aid of sunshine, higher plants are able to manufacture their own food. The structure of fungi is very simple; that is, it has not become highly differentiated or specialized as in flowering plants. Fungi have very simple physiological processes and are incapable of manufacturing their own food, but live as parasites or saprophytes, appropriating food already prepared by higher forms of plants. Occurring as parasites, they are responsible for extensive losses to agricultural crops and produce blights, rots, unsightly growths, rusts and smuts of grain, and diseases of ornamental and forest trees. Injuries from fungi are not confined entirely to plants but are sometimes the cause of disease in man and in animals.

One of the great advantages pertaining to the study of fungi as a hobby or diversion is that their occurrence, unlike that of many other plants, is not limited to a short calendar period but extends practically throughout the entire year. The appearance and abundance of mushrooms are subject to great variation, largely depending on weather conditions. This variation is influenced not only by the weather of the current season but also by that of the preceding year. Two important factors in the growth of fungi are heat and moisture. If the preceding year has been excessively dry, the underground or vegetative part of the fungus, known as the mycelium, and the minute reproductive bodies, known as spores, may have dried up or at least suffered a loss of vitality that would retard or discourage the appearance of many fungi the following season. On the contrary, a hot but wet season is highly conducive to the abundant production of mushrooms. The almost phenomenal appearance of fungous growths under such conditions has led to the stories of the seemingly miraculous appearance of mushrooms overnight. That fungi develop very rapidly is partly explained by the fact that much of the tissue is formed before the fungus breaks through the surface of the soil. In addition, fungous tissue is especially adapted to the rapid absorption of water, and as a result the growing plant expands very rapidly.

As already mentioned, fungi exhibit a remarkable diversity in size, form, and color. They vary from microscopic organisms, many of which cause plant diseases, to the large woody growths present on many injured or dying forest trees. In form or structure they range from very simple 1-celled structures to the fantastic complicated stinkhorn fungi. (Fig. 45.) The greatest variation in color may also be observed. In some species the colors are often very unobtrusive and quiet, while in other species they are striking in their diversity and brilliancy.

One very striking phenomenon exhibited by certain fungi is luminosity or phosphorescence. This character, while confined to a comparatively few fungi, is so striking or ghostlike as to have furnished material for fairy stories and among the natives of certain countries the basis for many superstitions. An Australian species is recorded as giving out such a clear emerald-green light that reading in the near vicinity is possible. Phosphorescence or luminosity is often observed in dead wood and is due to the presence of mycelium, the threadlike vegetative part of the fungus. This often gives off a bright glow which may be seen from some distance. Phosphorescence is often exhibited by the mushroom itself, as in the case of *Clitocybe illudens*, commonly known as jack-o'-lantern, and *Panus stypticus*, a very common and cosmopolitan species.

While the utilitarian value of mushrooms and certain other fungi is popularly thought to be very limited and mostly restricted to their use as food, there are many other uses, though not of universal practice, which may be mentioned. In early times various species were employed extensively in medicine, though to-day their use is rather restricted. Certain species were used as emetics, purgatives, astringents, or for their styptic property. Although the use of fungi in medicine is more restricted than in ancient times they still play an important rôle in various industries. Certain species are highly important as fermenting agents and are used in the manufacture of beer, wine, cider, vinegar, saki, alcohol, bread, cheese, and other commercial products. They have also been employed in the arts as tinder and for dyeing silks, cottons, and wool.

The main discussion of this circular is concerned with the class of fungi known as mushrooms, though a few interesting and conspicuous varieties of other groups are considered. The characters of each family or genus are discussed, and then descriptions of the plants belonging to the respective family or genus are given.

DANGER FROM POISONOUS FUNGI

On account of the many casualties resulting from the use of fungi as food by persons unfamiliar with the different kinds, an urgent appeal is made to the collector to abstain from experimenting with or eating any mushrooms unless he is absolutely certain of the identity and edibility of the species collected. It is not safe to collect young, unopened mushrooms, commonly known as buttons, as it is often difficult to distinguish between poisonous and edible species in the early stages.

Attention is called to the danger of depending on so-called tests for distinguishing poisonous and edible species. The assertions that mushrooms are poisonous if a silver coin placed in the utensil in which the mushrooms are cooked tarnishes, and that those which peel easily are edible, are wholly erroneous. The presence of insects on fungi is no guide as to their edibility, because insects infest both poisonous and edible mushrooms. The notion that soaking or boiling poisonous mushrooms in salt water will render them harmless has no foundation in fact.

Although it is quite possible for a person to learn a few common and characteristic mushrooms, this circular in no way guarantees that the reader may be able to distinguish between all edible and poisonous species, for in order to become thoroughly familiar with the subject, continued study under a competent instructor is absolutely necessary.

AGARICACEAE (GILL FUNGI)

Plants of the family Agaricaceae (gill fungi) have a well-defined stem or stipe, which bears an expanded portion known as the cap or pileus. On the lower surface of the cap are platelike structures known as gills or lamellae, on which the spores are borne. (Fig. 1.)

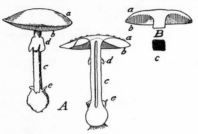

FIGURE 1.—A, A gill-bearing mushroom: *a,* Pileus or cap; *b,* gills; *c,* stem; *d,* ring; *e,* volva or cup. B, A tube-bearing or pore-bearing mushroom (section of upper part) : *a,* Cap; *b,* tubes or pores; *c,* view of part of lower side of cap

The manner in which the gills are attached to the stem is of great importance in determining species and should be carefully noted in the field. The best method of determining the manner of attachment is to cut the mushroom longitudinally through the cap, thus exposing the point of attachment of the gills and stem. The terms descriptive of this attachment may be best understood by referring to Figure 2.

If the mature mushroom is shaken, a fine powder may be seen falling from the gills. This powder consists of thousands of spores, which, through the agency of the wind, birds, or insects, are widely distributed. The color of the gills is a very important character in the determination of mushrooms and depends upon the color of the spores, which may be white, cream, yellowish, rose, brown, black, or purplish. The color may be conveniently determined by making a spore print as follows:

Cut the stem off close to the cap and place the cap, gill side down, on a piece of paper. Ordinary white paper will serve the purpose unless the mushroom has white or light-colored spores, in which case a colored paper will be more satisfactory. Spores so collected consti-

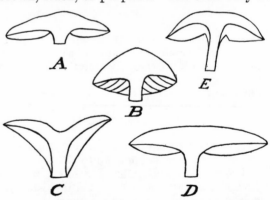

FIGURE 2.—Mushrooms showing varying shapes of caps and kinds of gills : A, Cap umbonate, gills free ; B, cap convex ; C, cap funnelform, gills decurrent ; D, cap expanded ; E, gills emarginate

tute a spore print and may be made permanent by spraying them with a solution of white shellac in alcohol. A saturated solution should be made and then diluted to 50 per cent with alcohol.

The stem is often an important diagnostic character; therefore careful descriptive field notes should be made of its color, size, shape, and texture.

In the early stages of development of certain genera and species the gills are covered with a membrane known as the veil, extending from the margin of the pileus to the stem. This veil may entirely disappear as the mushroom expands, or it may persist as a definite or cobwebby ring around the stem or as a fragmentary or cobwebby veil on the margin of the cap.

In the early stages of some genera the entire plant is inclosed in an envelope known as the volva. The manner in which this envelope breaks is of great importance in identifying species and should be carefully noted at the time the collection is made. In some cases it remains at the base of the plant as a complete or fragmentary cup or sheath, or as ridges on the lower part of the stem, or as scales on the top of the cap.

KEY TO AGARICACEAE [3]

The following key will be found a convenient means of distinguishing between the different genera of Agaricaceae. It will be observed that the first character to be considered is the color of the spores. This may be easily determined by using the method explained on page 4. Further points of difference are to be found in the presence or absence of the volva or of the veil, in the shape of the pileus, attachment of the gills, shape and marking of the stem, manner of growth, habitat, or some other distinguishing feature.

WHITE-SPORED AGARICS

Plants soft or more or less fleshy, soon decaying, not reviving well when moistened:

Ring or volva or both present— *Genus*

Volva and ring both present_____ AMANITA.

Volva present, ring absent_____ AMANITOPSIS.

Volva absent, ring present—

Gills free from stem_____ LEPIOTA.

Gills attached to the stem_____ ARMILLARIA.

Ring and volva both absent—

Stem excentric or lateral_____ PLEUROTUS.

Stem central—

Gills decurrent—

Edge blunt, foldlike, forked_____ CANTHARELLUS.

Edge thin, stem fibrous outside_____ CLITOCYBE.

Edge thin, stem cartilaginous outside_____ OMPHALIA.

Gills sinuate, general structure fleshy_____ TRICHOLOMA.

Gills adnate or adnexed—

Cap rather fleshy, margin incurved when young_____ COLLYBIA.

Cap thin, margin of cap at first straight, mostly bell-shaped _____ MYCENA.

Cap fleshy, gills very rigid and brittle, stem stout—

Milk present_____ LACTARIUS.

Milk absent_____ RUSSULA.

Gills various, often decurrent, adnate or only adnexed, edge thin, thick at junction of cap, usually distant, waxy_____ HYGROPHORUS.

Plants coriaceous, tough, fleshy, or membranaceous, reviving when moistened:

Stem generally central, substance of cap noncontinuous with that of stem, gills thin, often connected by veins or ridges_____ MARASMIUS.

Stem central, excentric, lateral, or absent, substance of cap continuous with that of stem—

Edge of gills toothed or serrate_____ LENTINUS.

Edge of gills not toothed or serrate_____ PANUS.

Edge of gills split into two laminæ and revolute____ SCHIZOPHYLLUM.

Plants corky or woody, gills radiating_____ LENZITES.

---

[3] See the Glossary, p. 58, for definitions of technical terms.

ROSY-SPORED AGARICS

Genus

Stem excentric or absent and pileus lateral_____ CLAUDOPUS
Stem central:
    Volva present, annulus wanting_____ VOLVARIA
    Volva and annulus absent—
        Cap easily separating from stem, gills free_____ PLUTEUS
        Cap confluent with stem, gills sinuate_____ ENTOLOMA.

OCHER-SPORED AGARICS (SPORES YELLOW OR BROWN)

Gills easily separable from flesh of cap:
    Margin of cap incurved, gills more or less decurrent forked
        or connected with veinlike reticulations_____ PAXILLUS.
Gills not easily separable from flesh of cap:
    Universal veil present, arachnoid_____ CORTINARIUS.
    Universal veil absent—
        Ring present_____ PHOLIOTA.
        Ring absent—
            Stem central—
                Cap turned in_____ NAUCORIA.
                Cap not turned in_____ GALERA.
            Stem excentric or none_____ CREPIDOTUS.

PURPLE-BROWN SPORED AGARICS

Cap easily separating from stem, gills usually free_____ AGARICUS.
Cap not easily separating from stem, gills attached:
    Ring present_____ STROPHARIA.
    Ring absent, veil remaining attached to margin of cap___ HYPHOLOMA.

BLACK-SPORED AGARICS

Gills deliquescing, cap thin, ring present in some species_____ COPRINUS.
Gills not deliquescing:
    Margin of cap striate, gills not variegated_____ PSATHYRELLA.
    Margin of cap not striate, gills variegated_____ PANAEOLUS.

AMANITA

The most poisonous fungi belong to the genus Amanita. Although it contains some edible species, the surest way to avoid danger is to let all species of the genus alone. A fungus of this kind may be recognized among the white-spored agarics by the presence of a volva and a veil. Young plants are completely inclosed by the volva, and the manner in which it breaks away varies according to the species. A part of the volva may remain on the top of the cap, around its margin as scales, or as a broken cup at the base of the stem.

AMANITA PHALLOIDES. DEATH CUP. (POISONOUS)

(Fig. 3)

In the death cup the color of the cap ranges from white or lemon to olive or brownish. It is broadly bell-shaped or oval and finally expanded, smooth or with patches of scales. In moist weather it is very sticky. The gills are free and white and the stem mostly smooth and bulbous, surrounded by the large cup-shaped volva. The ring is large, white, and reflexed.

The death cup is the most dangerous of all mushrooms. It is widely distributed and of very common occurrence and may be found growing in woods or cultivated land from spring until late autumn.

AMANITA MUSCARIA. FLY AGARIC
(POISONOUS)

(Fig. 4)

In the fly agaric the color of the cap ranges from yellow to orange or blood red, and the remnants of the volva remain as whitish scales on the cap. The veil persists as a large, torn ring about the upper part of the stem, which is white and enlarged at the base and usually marked by scaly ridges or incomplete rings.

This species may be found during the summer and fall, occurring singly or in small associations or in patches of considerable size. It grows in cultivated soil, on partially cleared land, and in woods or on roadsides. It does not demand a rich soil, but rather exhibits a preference for poor ground. The color is an exceedingly variable character, the plants being brighter colored when young and fading as they mature. A very pale-colored variety is often found in the late autumn.

This is a very poisonous species and is responsible for many deaths and numerous cases of severe poisoning. While its chief poisonous principle is muscarine, a second poisonous principle is believed to be present.

FIGURE 3.—*Amanita phalloides.* (Poisonous)

FIGURE 4.—*Amanita muscaria.* (Poisonous)

AMANITA CAESAREA. CAESAR'S MUSHROOM

(Fig. 5)

In this species the cap is hemispherical, smooth, and with a conspicuous striate margin. It is reddish or orange in color, later becoming yellow. The gills are free and yellow; the stem is yellow, cylindrical, only slightly enlarged at the base, attenuated upward, scaly below the annulus, and smooth above; the ring is yellow, large, membranaceous, and hangs like a collar from the upper part of the stem; and the volva is saclike and conspicuous, white as contrasted with the yellow of the stem.

This species is variously known as Caesar's agaric, royal agaric, orange Amanita, etc. It has been highly esteemed as an article of diet since the time of the early Greeks. It is particularly abundant during rainy weather and may occur solitary, several together, or in definite rings. Although *Amanita caesarea* is edible, great caution should always be used in order not to confuse it with poisonous Amanitas.

AMANITA STROBILIFORMIS. FIR-CONE AMANITA

(Fig. 6)

In this species the cap is convex or nearly plane, white or sometimes slightly cinereous on the disk, and covered with large, angular, pyramidal warts; the margin extends slightly beyond the gills and sometimes bears fragments of the ring, which is large and torn; the gills are broad and white; the stem is thick and white, floccose scaly, and the bulb very large with concentric-marginate ridges and furrows and abruptly pointed below.

This species is to be found in woods in midsummer and early fall and occurs solitary or two or three together. It is conspicuous because of its startling white color, the size of the cap, which varies from 4 to 10 inches, and the length of the stem, which ranges from 3 to 8 inches and terminates in a large bulb. This plant is not to be recognized as an edible species.

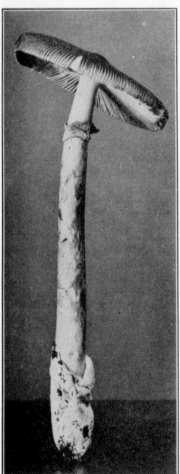

FIGURE 5.—*Amanita caesarea*

AMANITOPSIS

The genus Amanitopsis has white spores and a volva like Aminita but differs from it in the absence of a veil or a ring. The volva is large and persistent and at first completely envelops the young plant. As the latter matures it bursts through the volva, particles of which are carried up on the pileus in the form of delicate scales or flakes, which, however, are soon brushed off, leaving the pileus smooth.

Great care must be exercised to distinguish species of Amanitopsis from those of Amanita from which the ring has disappeared.

AMANITOPSIS VAGINATA.   SHEATHED AMANITOPSIS

(Fig. 7)

In this species the cap is thin and fragile, ovate to bell-shaped, sometimes umbonate, gray, mouse colored, or brown, smooth, shining, margin striate; the gills are white, broad, free; the stem is slender, fragile, smooth, or mealy, not bulbous; the volva is sheathing, white, easily separable from the stem, often remaining in the ground.

FIGURE 6.—*Amanita strobiliformis*

This is a very common and widely distributed species both in America and in Europe and is subject to great variation in size, color, and habitat. It may be found in woods, shaded situations, lawns, and sometimes on decaying wood.

LEPIOTA

The genus Lepiota may be distinguished from Amanita and Amanitopsis by the presence of a ring and the absence of a volva. The cap is generally scaly or granular, and the stem is fleshy and easily separable from the cap, in which it leaves a cuplike depression. The gills are usually free and are white when young, but certain species are pink or green when mature. The ring may be fixed or free, and when the plant is young it is readily seen, but before

FIGURE 7.—*Amanitopsis vaginata.* (From G. F. Atkinson)

maturity it may have disappeared. This genus contains some of the finest edible species as well as some extremely dangerous ones.

LEPIOTA PROCERA. PARASOL MUSHROOM. (EDIBLE)

(Fig. 8)

In the parasol mushroom the cap is ovate, then expanded with a distinct, smooth, brown umbo, the cuticle early breaking up into brown scales showing the white flesh; the gills are broad, crowded, white, free, and distant from the stem; the stem is tubular, long, bulbous, generally scaly or spotted, its substance distinct and free from the cap, in which a cavity is left by its removal; the ring is large and thick, readily movable when old.

The cap is 3 to 6 inches broad; the stem is 5 to 12 inches long and about 6 lines thick.

This very attractive and graceful species may be collected in pastures, lawns, gardens, thin woods, or roadsides. It occurs singly or scattered, appearing during summer and early fall, and is considered an excellent edible species.

LEPIOTA MORGANI. GREEN GILL. (POISONOUS)

(Fig. 9)

In this species the cap is fleshy, globose when young, expanded to plane or slightly depressed, not umbonate, white with a yellowish or brownish cuticle, which breaks up into scales except in the center; the flesh is white, generally changing to reddish or yellowish on being cut or bruised; the gills are close, lanceolate, remote, white becoming green; the stem is firm, smooth, hollow,

FIGURE 8.—*Lepiota procera.*   (Edible.)   (From C. G. Lloyd)

subbulbous, tapering upward, white with brownish tinge; the ring is large, movable.

The cap is 5 to 9 or even 12 inches broad; the stem is 6 to 9 inches long and 4 to 8 lines thick.

Great care should be taken to avoid this species.   Many instances of poisoning are well substantiated, and extreme inconvenience and serious illness have resulted from eating very small pieces of the uncooked mushroom.   The gills are slow in assuming the green tinge characteristic of the species, but after being allowed to remain several hours in ordinary room temperature the color becomes quite noticeable.

This fungus appears mostly on grassy places, such as lawns and parks, during the summer months, frequently forming large "fairy rings."

LEPIOTA NAUCINA. SMOOTH LEPIOTA

(Fig. 10)

In this species the cap is smooth, white or smoky, almost globose when young, then convex, expanding, and becoming somewhat gibbous; the flesh is white;

FIGURE 9.—*Lepiota morgani.* (Poisonous)

the gills are free from the stem, crowded, white, becoming smoky pink when old; the stem is rather stout, enlarged below, nearly hollow or loosely stuffed; the ring adheres to the stem.

The cap is 1½ to 3 inches broad; the stem is 2 to 3 inches long and 4 to 8 lines thick.

Peck[4] describes and discusses a form closely allied to *Lepiota naucina* which he calls *L. naucinoides,* the differences consisting in the smoother cap and in the shape of the spores. This latter character, being a microscopic feature, is of no practical assistance to the amateur.

These two forms are both considered edible, but extreme caution must be used in order not to collect poisonous or deadly white Amanitas for specimens of Lepiota before the pink tinge of the gills is apparent.

---

[4] PECK, CHARLES H.   35th Ann. Report of the New York State Museum of Nat. Hist., pp. 160–161. 1884.

LEPIOTA AMERICANA. AMERICAN LEPIOTA. (EDIBLE)

(Fig. 11)

In this species the cap is ovate, then convex, expanded, umbonate, the umbo and scales reddish brown; the flesh is white, becoming reddish if cut or bruised; the gills are white, ventricose, close, free; the stem is white, hollow, smooth,

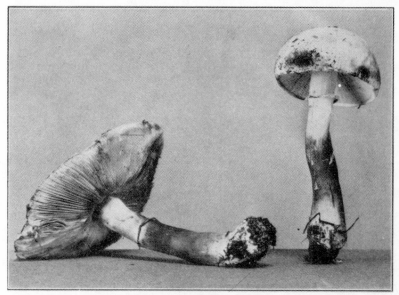

FIGURE 10.—*Lepiota naucina*

FIGURE 11.—*Lepiota americana.* (Edible)

swollen near the base, tapering above; the ring is rather large and delicate, and consequently it may disappear in old age.

The cap is 2 to 4 inches broad; the stem is 2 to 4 inches long and 3 to 5 lines thick.

This mushroom is of wide geographic distribution and grows singly or in clusters, often at the base of stumps, sometimes on sawdust piles, and again on grassy lawns. The plants are white when young, with the exception of the umbo and the scales, but in drying become smoky red. They are sometimes erect but frequently more or less ascending. *Lepiota americana* may be easily recognized by the peculiarity of turning red when bruised or old.

ARMILLARIA

Armillaria is another white-spored genus having a ring and no volva. The gills are attached to the stem and are sinuate or more or less decurrent. The substance of the stem and cap is continuous and firm. This genus may be distinguished from Amanita and Lepiota by the continuity of the substance of the stem and cap, and it is further differentiated from Amanita by the absence of a volva. *Armillaria mellea* is a common edible species.

ARMILLARIA MELLEA. HONEY-COLORED MUSH-ROOM. (EDIBLE)

(Fig. 12)

In *Armillaria mellea* the cap is oval to convex and expanded, sometimes with a slight elevation, smooth, or adorned with small pointed dark-brown or blackish scales, especially in the center, honey color to dull reddish brown, margin even or somewhat striate when old; the gills are adnate or decurrent, white or whitish, sometimes with reddish-brown spots; the stem is elastic, spongy, sometimes hollow, smooth or scaly, generally whitish, sometimes gray or yellow above the ring, below reddish brown.

FIGURE 12.—*Armillaria mellea.* (Edible)

The cap is 1½ to 6 inches broad; the stem is 2 to 6 inches long and one-half to three-fourths inch thick.

The species is extremely common and variable. It grows in large clusters about the base of rotten stumps and is often a serious parasite of fruit and shade trees. Both ring and stem are subject to marked variations. The former may be thick or thin or entirely absent, and the latter uniform in diameter or bulbous. The species is edible, though not especially tender or highly flavored.

On account of the great variation in color, surface of the cap, and shape of the stem, several forms of *Armillaria mellea* have been given varietal distinction. The following varieties as distinguished by Peck may be of assistance to the amateur:

Armillaria mellea var. *flava*, with yellow or reddish yellow cap.
Armillaria mellea var. *radicata*, with a tapering root.
Armillaria mellea var. *albida*, with white or whitish cap.

ARMILLARIA VENTRICOSA

(Fig. 13)

In this species the cap is fleshy, convex or nearly plane, smooth, shining white, margin thin and involute; the flesh is whitish; the gills are narrow and close, decurrent, sometimes dentate or denticulate on the edge, whitish; the

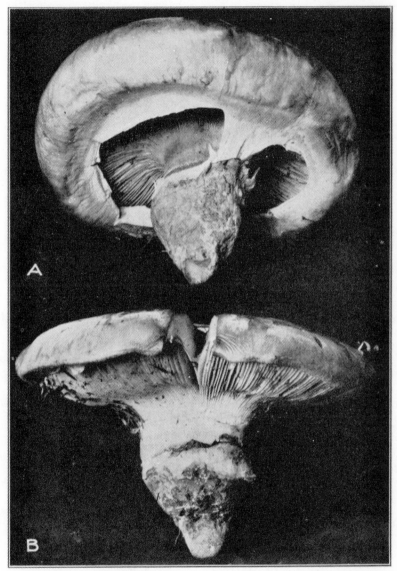

FIGURE 13.—*Armillaria ventricosa:* A, Young specimen; B, mature specimen

stem is thick and short, ventricose, abruptly pointed at the base; the ring is conspicuous, lacerated, and membranaceous.

The cap is 4 to 7 inches broad; the stem is 2 to 3 inches long, ventricose portion 1 to 2 inches broad.

This is a coarse, conspicuous fungus. It is not reported as widely distributed.

PLEUROTUS

The genus Pleurotus is chiefly distinguished among the white-spored agarics by the excentric stem or resupinate cap. The stem is fleshy and continuous with the substance of the cap, but it is subject to great variation in the different species and may be excentric, lateral, or entirely absent. The gills are decurrent or sometimes adnate, edge acute. Most of the species grow on wood, buried roots, or decayed stumps. The genus corresponds to Claudopus of the

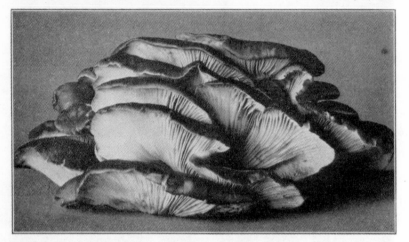

FIGURE 14.—*Pleurotus ostreatus.* (Edible)

pink-spored and Crepidotus of the brown-spored forms. The best-known species of this genus is the oyster mushroom.

PLEUROTUS OSTREATUS. OYSTER MUSHROOM. (EDIBLE)

(Fig. 14)

In the oyster mushroom the cap is either sessile or stipitate, shell shaped or dimidiate, ascending, fleshy, soft, smooth, moist, in color white, cream, grayish to brownish ash; the stem is present or absent (if present, short, firm, elastic, ascending, base hairy); the gills are white, decurrent, somewhat distant, anastomosing behind to form an irregular network.

The cap is 3 to 5 inches broad; mostly cespitose imbricated.

This is a very fine edible species of cosmopolitan distribution growing on limbs or trunks of living or dead trees, and appearing from early summer until late fall.

PLEUROTUS SAPIDUS. SAPID MUSHROOM. (EDIBLE)

This species very closely resembles *Pleurotus ostreatus* but is distinguished from it by the lilac-tinged spores, a characteristic difficult or impossible for the amateur to detect. From the gastronomic point of view these two species are equally attractive.

CANTHARELLUS

In the genus Cantharellus the cap is fleshy or submembranaceous, continuous with the stem, the margin entire, wavy, or lobed. The gills are decurrent, thick, narrow, blunt and foldlike, regularly forked, and connected by netlike veins. The two species discussed here are of common occurrence.

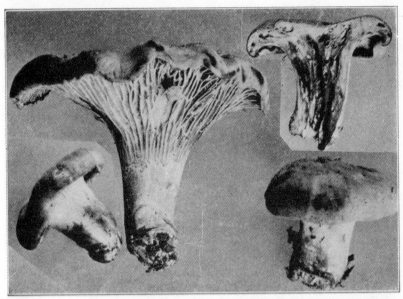

FIGURE 15.—*Cantharellus cibarius.*   (Edible)

CANTHARELLUS CIBARIUS.   THE CHANTERELLE.   (EDIBLE)

(Fig. 15)

In this species the cap is fleshy, thick, smooth, irregular, expanded, sometimes deeply depressed, opaque egg yellow, margin sometimes waxy; the flesh is

FIGURE 16.—*Cantharellus aurantiacus.*   (Suspected.)   (From G. F. Atkinson)

white; the gills are decurrent, thick, narrow, branching or irregularly connected, same color as cap; the stem is short, solid, expanding into a cap of the same color.

This is the famous chanterelle and has long been considered one of the best edible mushrooms. Ordinarily an agreeable odor of apricots may be observed, especially in the dried plants of this species. The chanterelle is of wide geographic distribution both in the United States and in Europe. It is a common summer species and may be found in grassy places, open or coniferous woods, gregarious or subcespitose.

CANTHARELLUS AURANTIACUS. FALSE CHANTERELLE. (SUSPECTED)

(Fig. 16)

In the false chanterelle the cap is fleshy, soft and somewhat silky, and dull orange to brownish; the shape is variable, convex, plane, or infundibuliform, the margin inrolled when young, later wavy or lobed; the flesh is yellowish; the gills are thin, decurrent, regularly forked and dark orange; the stem is spongy, fibrous, colored like the cap and larger at the base than at the top.

The use of this species for food is not to be recommended.

FIGURE 17.—*Clitocybe multiceps.* (Edible)

CLITOCYBE

The white-spored genus Clitocybe contains many species, some of which possess definite generic characters that render identification easy, while others are extremely difficult to recognize. The cap is generally fleshy, later in some species concave to infundibuliform, thinner at the margin, which is involute. The gills are adnate or decurrent. The stem is externally fibrous, tough, not readily separable from the flesh of the cap. The gills are never truly sinuate, a character separating Clitocybe from Tricholoma, with which it agrees in having a fibrous stem.

CLITOCYBE MONADELPHA. (EDIBLE)

In this species the cap is fleshy, convex, then depressed, at first smooth, later scaly, honey colored to pallid brownish or reddish; the gills are short, decurrent, flesh colored; the stem is elongated, twisted, crooked, fibrous, tapering at the base, pallid brownish.

This species bears a resemblance to *Armillaria mellea* but may be distinguished from it by the absence of a ring and by the decurrent gills. The plants are edible, but they soon become water-soaked and uninviting. They grow in large clusters in grass or about roots or stumps and are to be found from spring until late fall.

CLITOCYBE MULTICEPS.   MANY-HEADED CLITOCYBE.   (EDIBLE)

(Fig. 17)

In this species the cap is convex, fleshy, firm, thin except on the disk, slightly moist in wet weather, whitish, grayish, or yellowish gray, in young plants sometimes quite brown; the flesh is white, taste mild; the gills are white, close, adnate or somewhat decurrent; the stem is equal or little thickened, solid or stuffed, elastic, firm, somewhat pruinose at the apex.

The cap is 1 to 3 inches broad; the stem is 2 to 4 inches long.

This species is subject to great variation in size, color, shape of gills, texture, and taste. Sometimes the gills are very slightly sinuate, reminding one of the genus Tricholoma.

Clitocybe multiceps appears abundantly in the spring and autumn, growing in dense clusters often hidden by the grass or stubble. It is edible and by many considered very good.

FIGURE 18.—*Clitocybe ochropurpurea*

CLITOCYBE OCHROPURPUREA.   PURPLE-GILLED CLITOCYBE

(Fig. 18)

In this species the cap is subhemispherical to flat, in age upturned and irregular, pale yellow or yellowish tan, slightly changing to purple, smooth or somewhat hairy; the gills are adnate or decurrent, thick, broader behind, purple; the stem is solid, equal or swollen in center, conspicuously fibrous, paler in color than the pileus.

The cap is 2 to 4 inches broad; the stem is 2½ to 5 inches long.

Clitocybe ochropurpurea is to be found solitary or in small associations in grassy places and open woods, mixed or coniferous. It is coarse in appearance and sometimes attains a height of 6 inches. The decided purple of the gills makes it at first difficult for the amateur to recognize this species as belonging to the white-spored group, but a spore print will show the spores to be white or slightly cream.

CLITOCYBE DEALBATA. (SUSPECTED)

In this species the cap is convex, then plane, finally revolute and undulate, dry, even, smooth, somewhat shining; the flesh is thin, dry, white; the gills are adnate, crowded, scarcely decurrent, white; the stem is equal, erect, or ascending, stuffed, wholly fibrous, apex subpruinose.

While this species has been considered edible, it may easily be mistaken for *Clitocybe sudorifica*, a very dangerous fungus known as the "sweat-producing Clitocybe."

CLITOCYBE ILLUDENS. JACK-O'-LANTERN. (POISONOUS)

(Fig. 19)

In *Clitocybe illudens* the cap is fleshy, convex or expanded, then depressed, sometimes with a small umbo, saffron yellow, in age becoming sordid or brownish; the gills are broad, distant, and unequally decurrent; the stem is

FIGURE 19.—*Clitocybe illudens.* (Poisonous.) (From M. A. Williams)

solid, firm, smooth, and tapering toward the base, ascending, curved, rarely erect, color same as cap.

The cap is 4 to 6 inches broad; the stem is 5 to 8 inches long.

This is a very striking fungus on account of both its color and the large clumps it forms about stumps or decaying trees. It is often irregular in form, from the crowded habit of growth. On account of the phosphorescence which renders it conspicuous at night, it is commonly known as the jack-o'-lantern. While not considered a dangerous poisonous species, it produces illness and is to be carefully avoided. It may be found from August to October.

OMPHALIA

In the genus Omphalia the cap is generally thin, at first umbilicate, but later funnel shaped, with the margin either incurved or straight. The stem is cartilaginous, its flesh being continuous with that of the pileus but differing in character. Species of Omphalia are common on rotten wood on hilly slopes and are especially abundant in damp weather. Some species are extremely small.

This genus is closely related to Mycena and Collybia, but it is distinguished from them because of its decurrent gills.

OMPHALIA CAMPANELLA. BELL OMPHALIA.   (EDIBLE)

(Fig. 20)

In this species the cap is campanulate, sometimes expanded, umbilicate, smooth, hygrophanous, rusty yellow, slightly striate; the gills are narrow, arcuate, yellow, connected by veins, decurrent; the stem is slender, horny, smooth, hollow, brown, paler at apex, and hairy at base.

FIGURE 20.—*Omphalia campanella.*   (Edible)

The cap is four to eight lines broad; the stem is very slender and often ascending.

This little fungus may be found during the summer and fall. It is very common and widely distributed, growing on rotten logs in clusters or tufts, and exhibits a preference for coniferous wood. It is edible, tender, and of a fairly good flavor.

FIGURE 21.—*Tricholoma equestre.*   (Edible)

TRICHOLOMA

The genus Tricholoma is large and contains both edible and poisonous species, most of which are autumnal and terrestrial. The cap is fleshy, convex, never truly umbilicate or umbonate. A volva and a ring are wanting.   The gills are attached to the stem and are sinuate, the degree depending upon the particular species.   It has a fleshy fibrous stem, generally short and stout, the flesh of which is continuous with that of the cap.

TRICHOLOMA EQUESTRE.   EQUESTRIAN TRICHOLOMA.   (EDIBLE)

(Fig. 21)

In this species the cap is convex, becoming expanded, margin incurved at first, then slightly wavy, viscid, pale yellowish with a greenish or brownish tinge; the flesh· is white or slightly yellow; the gills are sulphur yellow, crowded, rounded behind, and· almost free; the stem is stout, solid, pale yellow, or white.

The cap is 2 to 3 inches broad; the stem is 1 to 2 inches long and one-half to three-fourths inch thick.

This species has a fairly wide geographic distribution and occurs very abundantly in Virginia, Maryland, and the District of Columbia from the middle of November until about Christmas.   It is to be found in pine woods, where it forms irregular or incomplete fairy rings.   The plants exert considerable force in pushing their way out of the ground through the dense mat of needles, which often adheres so closely to the caps that slight elevations are the only indications of the presence of the mushrooms.

Tricholoma equestre is a very excellent edible species and is delicious when fried or made into soup.   The latter resembles turkey soup, but possesses a more delicate flavor.

TRICHOLOMA TERREUM

In *Tricholoma terreum* the cap is fleshy, convex, or nearly plane, sometimes umbonate, innately fibrillose, floccose or scaly, grayish brown or mouse-colored; the flesh is white or light gray; the gills are subdistant, adnexed, white or ash colored; the stem is solid or hollow.

The cap is 1 to 3 inches broad; the stem is 1 to 2 inches long.

This species grows on the ground in mixed or coniferous woods.   It is found abundantly from· September to November, and much later in Virginia, Maryland, and the District of Columbia.

Tricholoma terreum frequently occurs in association with *T. equestre*, appearing in abundance when the season has been too dry for a good run of *T. equestre*.

TRICHOLOMA NUDUM.   (EDIBLE)

The entire plant of *Tricholoma nudum* is at first violaceous, becoming paler and sometimes reddish; the cap is convex, then expanded and sometimes depressed, moist, smooth, margin incurved, thin, naked, flesh-colored, comparatively thin, but firm and solid; the gills are crowded, rounded behind, and somewhat decurrent if cap is depressed, violet, but later may be reddish; the stem is equal, stuffed, violaceous, becoming pale.

The cap is 2 to 3 inches broad; the stem is 2 to 3 inches long and one-half inch thick.

This species is edible and very good.   The more delicate flavor of young plants makes them preferable to those in which the color changes have taken place.   It grows on rich ground among leaves and is mostly gregarious.

TRICHOLOMA PERSONATUM.   BLEWITS.   (EDIBLE)

(Fig. 22)

In this species the cap is convex, expanded, slightly depressed, fleshy, moist, pale tan, tinged gray or violet; young plants may be entirely violet, margin downy, involute; the flesh is whitish; the gills are crowded, rather broad, rounded behind, nearly free, violaceous, changing to dull reddish brown; the stem is stout, sub-bulbous, fibrillose, solid, colored like cap or lighter.

The cap is 2 to 5 inches broad; the stem is 1½ to 2½ inches long and one-half to three-fourths inch thick.

Tricholoma personatum is to be found quite commonly in the late summer and fall months growing on the ground in woods and open places. This is one of the most acceptable edible species.

Tricholoma personatum and *T. nudum* are often confusing to the amateur, but may be distinguished from each other by the fact that in *T. nudum* the margin of the cap is naked and is thinner than in *T. personatum*. Also *T. nudum* is more slender than *T. personatum* and has deeper coloration on the cap and gills.

TRICHOLOMA RUSSULA. RED TRICHOLOMA. (EDIBLE)

In *Tricholoma russula* the cap is convex, later plane, and sometimes depressed; disk granular, viscid in damp weather, red or flesh-colored, becoming lighter at the margin, which is involute and in young plants downy; the flesh is white or ringed with red under the cuticle, friable, taste mild; the gills are rounded or somewhat decurrent, rather distant, white, later becoming red spotted; the stem is solid, white, stained with red dots or squamules at the apex.

The cap is 3 to 5 inches broad; the stem is 1 to 3 inches long and one-half to three-fourths inch thick.

FIGURE 22.—*Tricholoma personatum.* (Edible)

This species is to be found in mixed woods and on hilly slopes from August until after frost. It may occur solitary, but often is found in patches. It is edible and reported of fine flavor.

There is frequently a sharp line of demarcation that appears like a well-defined encircling ridge between the gills and the upper part of the stem.

COLLYBIA

In the genus Collybia the volva and the veil are both absent. The margin of the cap is at first involute and the gills adnate, adnexed, and never decurrent; the stem is of different substance from the cap, fibrous or fistulose, cartilaginous or with a cartilaginous bark.

COLLYBIA RADICATA. ROOTED COLLYBIA. (EDIBLE)

(Fig. 23)

In the rooted Collybia the cap is convex to nearly plane, distinctly umbonate, often wrinkled, especially near the umbo, grayish brown or almost white, glutinous when moist, margin incurved when young, sometimes upturned when mature; the flesh is thin, white; the gills are white, broad, ventricose, dis-

FIGURE 23.—*Collybia radicata*.   (Edible)

tant, adnexed, sometimes notched b e h i n d ; the stem is smooth, striate, g r o o v e d or mealy, straight, slightly twisted, same color as the cap, but generally p a l e r, slightly tapering upward, and with a long, rooting base.

The cap is 1½ to 3 inches broad; the stem is 4 to 8 inches long and 3 to 5 lines thick.

The rooted Collybia may be found in woods or on shaded grassy places, either singly or in groups. The "root" may often be found attached to well-decayed roots of trees beneath the surface of t h e ground. It is readily recognized by the distinctive character of the gills and by the tapering pointed root which often greatly exceeds the stem in length. It has always been reported as edible.

COLLYBIA VELUTIPES. VEL-
  VET-STEMMED COLLYBIA.
  (EDIBLE)

(Fig. 24)

In this species the cap is convex, soon plane, sometimes irregular and excentric, smooth, viscid, tawny yellow, with margin probably lighter than the disk; the flesh is thick in the center, thin at the margin, soft, watery, white or yellowish; the gills are broad, rather distant, unequal, tawny or light

FIGURE 24.—*Collybia velutipes*.   (Edible.)   (From C. G. Lloyd)

yellow, rounded behind and slightly adnexed; the stem is tough, cartilagineus, densely velvety-villose, deep umber becoming black, equal or slightly enlarged at base, hollow or stuffed.

The cap is 1 to 3 inches broad; the stem is 1 to 3 inches long and 2 to 4 lines thick.

The velvet-stemmed Collybia is readily recognized by its dark villose stem and viscid cap, which in wet weather may even appear to have a thick, glutinous coat. It grows on ground that contains decaying wood, on stumps, or even on living trees, where the mycelium may have gained entrance through a wound. In such instances it assumes a semiparasitic habit, and considerable injury to the tree may result. Although *Collybia velutipes* is reported as occurring in every month of the year, it is especially a cold-weather species.

MYCENA

In the genus Mycena the cap is thin, conic or bell-shaped, and usually streaked with longitudinal lines. In some species it is blunt or umbonate when expanded. The margin is at first straight and closely applied to the stem. The gills are adnate or adnexed, and in some species there is a slight decurrent tooth.

FIGURE 25.—*Mycena galericulata.*   (Edible.)   (From G. F. Atkinson)

The plants are small, brittle, and often possess a strong alkaline odor or an odor of radishes, which, however, frequently disappears in drying. As the odor is not permanent, the collector should promptly note the character when the specimens are fresh.

The genera Collybia and Mycena are closely related but may be distinguished by the fact that in Collybia in the young condition the margin of the cap is inrolled while in Mycena it is straight and lies against the stem. In addition, in species of Mycena the cap is generally bell-shaped, and the stem is remarkably brittle and if broken quickly can be heard to snap.

MYCENA GALERICULATA.   (EDIBLE)
(Fig. 25)

In this species the cap is conical, bell-shaped, umbonate when expanded, dry and smooth, brownish gray, striate to the umbo; the gills are white to flesh-colored, adnate, slightly decurrent, rather distant, unequal, connected by veins; the stem hollow, rigid, polished, villose at base.

The cap is three-fourths to 1½ inches broad; the stem is 1 to 3 inches long and 2 lines thick.

This is an extremely variable species. Authors sometimes recognize three varieties, *longipes, expansus,* and *calopus.* The variety *longipes* is distinguished by the extreme length of the stem, *expansus* by the breadth and expansion of its cap, and *calopus,* the most attractive variety, by the chestnut-colored stem. The plants are common and abundant, generally growing in large clusters united by the downy hairs of the base of the stems. They are to be found on rotten logs or old stumps of various kinds of trees from March to November. Both caps and stems of young plants are reported edible and as possessing a delicate flavor.

LACTARIUS

The distinguishing feature of the genus Lactarius is the presence of a white or colored milk, especially abundant in the gills. The entire plant is brittle and inclined to rigidity. The fleshy cap is more or less depressed and frequently marked with concentric zones. The gills are often somewhat decurrent, but in certain species are adnate or adnexed, unequal in length, and often forked. The stem is stout, rigid, central, or slightly excentric.

Species of this genus are generally terrestrial, often of very large size, and occur in considerable number in open woods or thickets.

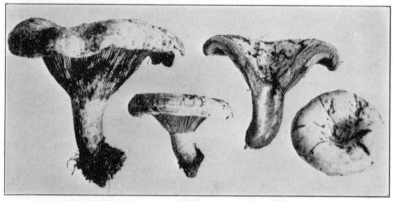

FIGURE 26.—*Lactarius indigo.* (Edible)

LACTARIUS DELICIOSUS.   DELICIOUS LACTARIUS.   (EDIBLE)

In this species the cap is convex but depressed in the center when quite young, finally funnel shaped, smooth, slightly viscid, deep orange, yellowish or grayish orange, generally zoned, margin naked, at first involute, unfolding as the plant becomes infundibuliform; the flesh is soft, pallid; the gills are crowded, narrow, often branched, yellowish orange; the stem is equal or attenuated at the base, stuffed, then hollow, of the same color as the cap except that it is paler and sometimes has dark spots.

The cap is 2 to 5 inches broad; the stem is 1 to 2 inches long and 1 inch thick.

This fungus is distinctive on account of its orange color and the concentric zones of light and dark orange on the cap and because of its saffron red or orange milk. A peculiarity of the plant is that it turns green upon bruising and in age changes from the original color to greenish. It is widely distributed and of common occurrence, appearing on the ground in woods, solitary or in patches, from June or July to October.

This species has long been highly prized as an article of food and is thought to have been referred to by Pliny. A picture supposed to be this species has been found in a mural decoration in Pompeii.

LACTARIUS INDIGO.   INDIGO LACTARIUS.   (EDIBLE)
(Fig. 26)

In this species the cap at first is umbilicate and the margin involute, later depressed or infundibuliform with margin elevated, indigo blue with a silvery gray luster, zonate, fading in age, becoming greenish and less distinctly zoned, milk abundant and dark blue; the gills are crowded, indigo blue, changing to greenish in age; the stem is short, nearly equal, hollow.

This mushroom may be very easily recognized by the striking blue color of the cap and milk. It occurs in mixed or coniferous woods, singly or in small associations, in summer and autumn.

RUSSULA

The genus Russula is similar to Lactarius in form, brittleness, and general appearance, but differs in the absence of milk. The species are very abundant in the summer, extending into the fall months. Many species are regarded as edible, but several are known to be poisonous; therefore it is advisable to abstain from eating any members of this genus.

RUSSULA EMETICA. EMETIC RUSSULA. (POISONOUS)

In this species the cap is oval to bell-shaped, becoming flattened or depressed, smooth, shining, rosy to dark red when old, fading to tawny, sometimes becoming yellow, margin finally furrowed and tuberculate; the flesh is white,

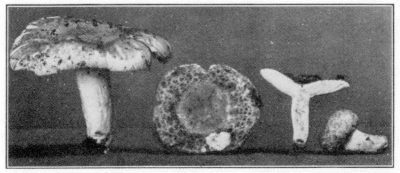

FIGURE 27.—*Russula virescens.* (Edible)

but reddish under the separable pellicle; the gills are nearly free, somewhat distant, shining white; taste is very acrid; the stem is stout, spongy-stuffed, fragile when old, white or reddish.

The cap is 3 to 4 inches broad; the stem is 2½ to 3 inches long.

This is a very attractive plant but is exceedingly acrid and poisonous. It occurs during the summer and autumn on the ground in woods or open spaces.

RUSSULA VIRESCENS. GREEN RUSSULA. (EDIBLE)
(Fig. 27)

In this species the cap is at first rounded, then expanded, when old somewhat depressed in the center, dry, green, the surface broken up into quite regular, more or less angular areas of deeper color, margin straight, obtuse, even; the gills are adnate, somewhat crowded, equal or forked; the stem is equal, thick, solid, or spongy, rivulose, white.

The cap is 3½ to 5 inches broad; the stem is about 2 inches long.

This fungus is noticeable on account of the color and areolate character of the cap. In Virginia, Maryland, and the District of Columbia it occurs usually from July to September, either solitary or in small patches, but not in very great abundance. The species is edible and of good flavor.

HYGROPHORUS

In the genus Hygrophorus the cap is viscid, moist, or hygrophanous, and the flesh is continuous with that of the stem. The cap may be regular but is often plicate or folded and the margin irregular, wavy, and lobed. The gills are generally distant, adnexed, adnate, or decurrent, thick with acute edge, watery, and of waxy consistency. The latter characteristic may be easily demonstrated by rubbing a bit of the gills between the fingers. Hygrophorus is closely related to Cantharellus, the gills of which are blunt and forked but never waxy.

HYGROPHORUS CHRYSODON.   GOLDEN-TOOTH HYGROPHORUS.   (EDIBLE)

In this species the cap is fleshy, convex, then expanded, margin involute when young, viscid, shining when dry, white, with scattered golden squamules; the gills are white, distant, decurrent; the stem stuffed, soft, nearly equal, white, with minute yellow squamules, more numerous toward the apex, where they are often arranged in the form of a ring.

The cap is 2 to 3 inches broad; the stem is 2 to 3 inches long.

This plant is easily recognized on account of the golden granules on the cap and stem. It grows on the ground in woods or open situations in the late summer and fall, but is not of very common occurrence.

HYGROPHORUS COCCINEUS.   SCARLET HYGROPHORUS

In this species the cap is convexo-plane, obtuse, hygrophanous, smooth, scarlet, becoming yellowish in age, fragile, generally unequal; the gills are adnate, decurrent with a tooth, distant, connected by veins, light yellow in the middle, purplish at the base when mature; the stem is hollow, then compressed, base always yellow, scarlet upward.

The cap is 1 to 2 inches broad; the stem is about 2 inches long.

This species occurs in moist places and on mossy banks.

HYGROPHORUS CONICUS.   CONIC HYGROPHORUS.   (POISONOUS)

In this species the cap is strikingly conical, yellow, orange, scarlet, margin often lobed; the gills are free or adnate, rather loose and broad, yellow; the stem is equal, hollow, fibrous striate, yellow or scarlet.

The cap is one-half to 1 inch broad; the stem is 3 to 4 inches long.

This is a very attractive little fungus on account of its bright color and symmetrical conical cap. A very distinctive character is the blackening of the fungus in drying. It occurs on the ground in rich woods and in damp places near streams from August to September or later.

HYGROPHORUS HYPOTHEJUS.   (EDIBLE)

In this species the cap is convex, somewhat depressed, at first covered with an olivaceous slime, after its disappearance ash colored, pale yellow, orange, or often rufescent; the flesh is thin, white, becoming light yellow; the gills are decurrent, distant, whitish or pallid, later yellow or flesh-colored; the stem is equal, viscid, stuffed, becoming hollow, paler than the cap.

The cap is 1½ inches broad; the stem is 2 or more inches long.

This is an interesting little species, occurring late in the fall in pine woods after most of the mushrooms have disappeared. The partial veil is floccose, but early fugacious, and is of such a transitory character that it is of very little value to the amateur in identifying the species. It is edible, though not especially adapted to cooking, but when dried it is nutty and fairly palatable.

MARASMIUS

In the genus Marasmius the plants are dry, thin, tough, and membranaceous. They are characterized by their habit of shriveling and drying up in dry weather and reviving in wet weather. The gills are dry, almost membranaceous, often narrow, distant, and connected by veins. The stem is cartilaginous or horny and continuous with the cap.

Marasmius is closely related to Collybia, Lentinus, and Panus. Certain species have been described as belonging to Collybia and are especially difficult of identification. The majority of the species of Marasmius have a central stem, while the stem in Lentinus and Panus is variable, being central, excentric, lateral, or absent. Marasmius species are also much smaller than those of the other genera mentioned.

Species of Marasmius are found growing on the ground, wood, or rotting leaves. Several species are known to cause disease in economic plants such as sugarcane, banana, and cacao.

MARASMIUS OREADES. FAIRY-RING FUNGUS. (EDIBLE)

(Fig. 28)

In the fairy-ring mushroom the cap is convex, then plane and slightly umbonate, tough, smooth, brownish buff, later cream-colored, margin when moist may be striate; the gills are broad, free, distant, unequal, creamy white; the stem is tough, solid, equal, villose in the upper part, smooth at the base.

FIGURE 28.—*Marasmius oreades.* (Edible)

The cap is 1 to 2 inches broad; the stem is 2 to 3 inches long and 1½ lines thick.

Many allusions in literature undoubtedly refer to this interesting little mushroom and many fairy stories have happy association with it. Its frequent occurrences on grassy places, as lawns, pastures, and golf courses, insures its wide acquaintance. It is to be found from early spring until autumn. This is a popular edible species and if once learned should always be recognized. It may be preserved for winter use by drying, and it is also well adapted for pickling.

MARASMIUS ROTULA. THE COLLARED MUSHROOM

In this species the cap is white or pale yellowish and darker at the disk, papery, deeply furrowed, smooth, umbilicate; margin crenate; the gills are the color of the cap, distant, attached to a collar which surrounds the stem; the stem is threadlike, smooth, shining, hollow, blackish.

The cap is one-fourth or one-half inch broad; the stem is 1 to 1½ inches long.

This species is commonly found on leaves and twigs in forests. The species can be at once recognized by the gills being attached to a collar free from the stem.

LENTINUS

In the genus Lentinus the plants are tough, leathery, corky, becoming hard and almost woody when old. The cap is generally irregular in form, usually depressed, often scaly or velvety. The gills are slightly or deeply decurrent, unequal, thin with margin notched or serrate. In some species the stem is present and is central, excentric, or lateral; in other species it is absent. The plants are to be found on stumps or logs or rotting lumber.

LENTINUS LEPIDEUS. SCALY LENTINUS

(Fig. 29)

In the scaly Lentinus the cap is at first convex, later becoming more or less flattened, tan to yellow with coarse, brown, irregular, concentric scales, often

FIGURE 29.—*Lentinus lepideus.* (From F. E. Clements)

areolate; gills are decurrent, sinuate, white; when young covered by a veil; stem is central or excentric, whitish, mostly scaly, short, thick, hard, equal, or tapering at the base.

The cap is 2 to 4 inches broad; the stem is about 1 inch long.

This is a common untidy-looking species, growing on old stumps and railroad ties, in which it produces a serious decay. It is considered edible but is of doubtful flavor, and it soon becomes tough.

LENTINUS LECOMTEI. HAIRY LENTINUS

In this species the cap is funnel-shaped, regular or irregular with inrolled margin, tawny or reddish brown, tough, villose-velvety; the gills are pallid, narrow, and crowded, decurrent, the edges nearly entire; the stem is central, excentric, or lateral, hairy when young.

The cap is 1½ to 3½ inches broad; the stem is usually short.

This is a very common and widely distributed species. It is to be found in clumps on old stumps, logs, and dead branches from spring to autumn, although it persists throughout the winter.

PANUS

PANUS STYPTICUS.   BITTER PANUS.   (POISONOUS)

This little species might be taken for Lentinus because of its general appearance and character; by certain authors it has been considered as belonging to that genus.   However, in typical Lentinus species the gills are serrate, while in Panus they are entire.

The cap is pale cinnamon to light tan, kidney-shaped, scurfy, tough; the gills are thin, narrow, crowded, connected by veins; the stem is short, lateral, ascending, and pruinose.

The cap is one-half to 1 inch broad.

This is a very common species and is to be found in clusters on stumps. The phosphorescence of rotten stumps is often due to its presence.   It is shriveled and inconspicuous in dry weather, reviving in wet weather.

Panus stypticus is extremely astringent, producing a very uncomfortable condition of the mouth and throat.   It is furthermore considered poisonous.

CLAUDOPUS

The genus Claudopus belongs to the rosy-spored agarics and corresponds to Pleurotus of the white-spored agarics in the cap being excentric and lateral, the stem rudimentary or obsolete, and the gills sinuate or decurrent.   The plants grow in an inverted position upon stumps or old wood.

CLAUDOPUS NIDULANS.   NEST-CAP CLAUDOPUS

In this species the cap is suborbicular or kidney-shaped, sessile or narrowed behind into a stemlike base, caps often overlapping, yellow or buff, downy, hairy or scaly toward the involute margin; the gills are broad, rather close, orange yellow.

The cap is 1 to 3 inches broad.

Claudopus nidulans is widely distributed and is to be found in the fall, growing on decaying branches, wood, etc.   It is easily recognized from its shelving and sometimes resupinate habit, yellow or buff cap, and orange yellow gills.   It is edible, and though the taste is said to be mild and pleasant, the substance is tough.

VOLVARIA

The genus Volvaria is distinguished among the rosy-spored agarics by the universal veil, which, becoming ruptured, remains as a large loose cup at the base of the stem, and by the absence of a ring.   The stem is easily separable from the cap and the gills are usually free, rounded behind, at first white, but later pink.

The genus is comparable to Amanitopsis among the white-spored agarics in having a volva but no ring.   Species of Volvaria grow in rich woods, on leaf mold or rotten wood, and on richly manured ground.

VOLVARIA BOMBYCINA.   SILKY VOLVARIA

(Fig. 30)

In this species the cap is globose, bell-shaped, later convex and sometimes subumbonate, white, silky when young, smooth at the apex, sometimes scaly when old; the flesh is white; the gills are ventricose, free, not reaching the margin, edge sometimes toothed, the stem is white, solid, smooth, tapering from base to apex; the volva is large, membranaceous, tough, somewhat viscid.

The cap is 3 to 8 inches broad; the stem is 3 to 6 inches long and 6 lines thick.

This species is widely distributed, but nowhere common.   It is found on fallen or living trees of various species.

PLUTEUS

The genus Pluteus may be recognized among the rosy-spored agarics by its symmetrical cap, central stem distinct from the cap, and free salmon-colored gills. In addition to these features, the absence of a volva and ring will assist in the determination of the species of this genus.

These plants are usually found growing on decaying wood, lumber, and sawdust piles.

PLUTEUS CERVINUS. FAWN-COLORED PLUTEUS. (EDIBLE)

In this species the cap is at first bell-shaped, later convex and expanded to almost plane, fleshy, generally smooth but with radiating fibrils, or sometimes more or less scaly, light brown, or sooty; margin entire; the flesh is

FIGURE 30.—*Volvaria bombycina*

white; the gills are broad, ventricose, unequal, free, white becoming flesh-colored; the stem is color of cap, paler above, firm, solid, fibrillose or sub-glabrous, nearly equal but slightly tapering above.

The cap is 2 to 5 inches broad; the stem is 2 to 5 inches long and 3 to 6 lines thick.

Pluteus cervinus occurs intermittently from spring to early fall. It grows at the base of decaying stumps or logs and sometimes appears in great abundance on sawdust piles. It is edible, and when young it is tender and of good flavor.

PHOLIOTA

The genus Pholiota is distinguished among the ocher-spored agarics by the presence of an annulus which is membranaceous in character and persistent or fugacious. The cap is more or less fleshy, yellowish, tawny, and sometimes scaly. The gills are adnate or slightly decurrent by a tooth. This genus corresponds to Armillaria of the white-spored agarics.

PHOLIOTA ADIPOSA. FATTY PHOLIOTA. (EDIBLE)

(Fig. 31)

In this species the cap is firm, fleshy, subconical to convex, glutinous when moist, yellowish, brown in center, often torn into dark scales, margin incurved; the flesh is thick at the center, spongy, yellowish; the gills are close, adnate, sometimes notched, yellowish to rust color; the stem is firm, whitish to yellow, viscid, clothed with brownish scales below the slight, floccose ring.

The cap is 2 to 4 inches broad; the stem is 2 to 4 inches long and 4 to 6 lines thick.

This species, commonly known as the "fatty Pholiota," forms large clusters in the fall on trunks or crotches of trees or on stumps. It is a rather showy fungus, easily attracting attention because of its tufted habit of growth, yellow color, and conspicuous scales. *Pholiota adiposa* is considered edible by American authorities. but it is not especially good. With this particular species it is preferable to peel the cap preparatory to cooking. The season is mostly confined to the fall months.

FIGURE 31.—*Pholiota adiposa.* (Edible)

PHILIOTA CAPERATA. WRINKLED PHOLIOTA. (EDIBLE)

In this species the cap is fleshy, yellow to yellow brown, ovate, obtuse or plane when expanded, viscid when moist, sometimes covered with whitish tufts; the gills are adnate, crowded, narrow, may be serrate, yellowish brown; the stem is stout, solid, sometimes slightly enlarged at base, white and shining, scaly above the ring; the ring is membranaceous, broad.

The cap is 2½ to 4 inches broad; the stem is 3 to 5 inches long and one-half to over 1 inch thick.

This fungus appears in the fall quite abundantly in certain localities. The specific name refers to the wrinkled character of the pileus, a prominent and constant feature of the plant. It is edible, slightly acrid when raw, but fairly good when cooked.

PHOLIOTA MARGINATA. (SUSPECTED)

In this species the cap is convex, then expanded, obtuse to plane, smooth, hygrophanous, slightly fleshy, tan when dry, honey colored when moist, margin striate; the gills are adnate, crowded, narrow, when mature reddish brown; the stem is hollow, equal, smooth, or slightly fibrillose; color same as the cap, whitish velvety at base; ring often distant from apex of stem, soon disappearing.

The cap is one-half to 1 inch broad; the stem is 1 to 2 inches long and about 2 lines thick.

This attractive little fungus appears principally in the fall, but it may occur sparingly during the summer. It grows singly or clustered on rotten stumps or logs.

PHOLIOTA SQUARROSA. SCALY PHOLIOTA. (EDIBLE)

In this species the cap is yellowish brown, clothed with dark persistent scales, dry, convex, then flattened, sometimes obtusely umbonate or gibbous; the flesh is light yellow; the gills are crowded, narrow, adnate with a decurrent tooth, pale olive, then rust colored; the stem is stuffed, yellowish brown, with dense dark recurved scales below the ring, much thinner at base than apex; ring near the apex generally floccose, seldom membranaceous and entire.

The cap is 2 to 5 inches broad; the stem is 3 to 6 inches long.

This species occurs in many localities from the last of June until frost, growing on trunks of trees and stumps. It is conspicuous because of the large clusters and prominent scales on both cap and stem. The fungus is good when young, raw or cooked, and by some authorities is considered excellent.

CORTINARIUS

The genus Cortinarius is easily recognized when young among the ocher-spored agarics by the powdery gills and by the cobwebby veil, which is separable from the cuticle of the cap. In mature plants the remains of the veil may often be observed adhering to the margin of the cap and forming a silky zone on the stem. Cortinarius contains many forms which are difficult of specific determination. Many species are edible, some indifferent or unpleasant, and others positively injurious. The best advice to the amateur is to abstain from eating species of this genus. The colors are generally conspicuous and often very beautiful. Most of the species occur in the autumn.

CORTINARIUS CINNAMOMEUS. (EDIBLE)

In this species the cap is rather thin, conic campanulate, when expanded almost plane, but sometimes unbonate, yellow to bright cinnamon colored, with perhaps red stains, smooth, silky from innate, yellowish fibrils, sometimes concentric rows of scales near the margin; the flesh is yellowish; the gills are yellow, tawny, or red, adnate, slightly sinuate and decurrent by a tooth, crowded, thin, broad; the stem is equal, stuffed then hollow, yellowish, fibrillose.

The cap is 1 to 2½ inches broad; the stem is 2 to 4 inches long and 3 to 4 lines thick.

This is a very common and widely distributed species, particularly abundant in mossy coniferous woods from summer until fall. The color of the gills is an extremely variable character, ranging from brown or cinnamon to blood red. A form possessing gills of the latter color is known as *Cortinarius cinnamomeus* var. *semisanguineus*. This species and variety are edible and considered extremely good, but great care should be exercised in determining the species.

CORTINARIUS LILACINUS. (EDIBLE)

(Fig. 32)

In this species the cap is firm, hemispherical, then convex, minutely silky, lilac colored; the gills are close, violaceous changing to cinnamon; the stem is solid, stout, distinctly bulbous, silky fibrillose, whitish with a lilac tinge.

The cap is 2 to 3 inches broad; the stem is 2 to 4 inches long.

This is a comparatively rare but very beautiful mushroom and an excellent edible species. It is to be found in mossy or swampy places.

NAUCORIA

Another genus belonging to the ocher-spored agarics is Naucoria. In this genus the volva and veil are both absent, the cap is more or less fleshy, at first conical or convex with involute margin, and the gills are free or adnate but never decurrent.

NAUCORIA SEMIORBICULARIS. (EDIBLE)

In this species the cap is hemispherical, convex to expanded, smooth, even, slightly viscid when moist, corrugated or cracked when dry and old, tawny, rust colored; the gills are adnate, sometimes notched, crowded, pale, then rust colored; the stem is tough, slender, straight, equal, smooth, hollow, with a free fibrous tube, pale reddish brown, darker at the base.

The cap is 1 to 2 inches broad; the stem is 3 to 4 inches long.

This is one of the most common and widely distributed species. It is among the first to appear in the spring and continues until autumn, being particularly abundant in wet weather.

It is edible, easily cooked, and of fair flavor.

FIGURE 32.—*Cortinarius lilacinus.* (Edible)

GALERA

The plants of the genus Galera are slender and fragile. The cap is regular, thin, more or less membranaceous, conic or bell-shaped, often striate, especially when moist, margin straight, never incurved, as in Naucoria. The gills are adnate or adnexed. The stem is somewhat cartilaginous, hollow, and polished.

GALERA TENERA. (EDIBLE)

In this species the cap is conic or bell-shaped, rust colored when damp, ochraceous when dry, hygrophanous, membranaceous, smooth, but striate when damp; the gills are cinnamon, broad, ascending adnate; the stem is slender, fragile, smooth, sometimes striate, mealy above, paler than cap.

The cap is 5 lines to three-fourths inch broad; the stem is 2 to 4 inches long.

This little fungus is very common in lawns or in richly manured places, where it appears early in the spring and persists until frost. It exhibits considerable variation in size and color, the latter ranging from light tan to brown and depending upon conditions of humidity.

AGARICUS

The genus Agaricus is characterized by brown or blackish spores with a purplish tinge and by the presence of a ring. The cap is mostly fleshy and the gills are free from the stem. The genus is closely related to Stropharia, but is separated from it by the fact that it has free gills and by the noncontinuity of the stem and the cap. The species of Agaricus occur in pastures, meadows, woods, and manured ground. All are edible, but certain forms are of especially good flavor. Bright colors are mostly absent and white or dingy brown shades predominate.

AGARICUS ARVENSIS. HORSE OR FIELD MUSHROOM. (EDIBLE)

In this species the cap is convex, bell-shaped, then expanded, when young floccose or mealy, later smooth, white, or yellowish; the flesh is white; the gills white to grayish pink, at length blackish brown, free, close, may be broader toward the stem; the stem is stout, hollow or stuffed, may be slightly bulbous, smooth; the ring is rather large, thick, the upper part white, membranaceous, the lower yellowish and radially split.

The cap is 3 to 5 inches broad; the stem is 2 to 5 inches high, and 4 to 10 lines thick.

Agaricus arvensis is to be found in fields, pastures, and waste places. It is closely related to the ordinary cultivated mushroom, but differs in its larger size and double ring. It is an excellent edible species, the delicacy of flavor and texture largely depending, like other mushrooms, upon its age.

AGARICUS SILVICOLA. FOREST MUSHROOM. (EDIBLE)

In this species the cap is convex, expanded to almost plane, sometimes umbonate, smooth, shining, white, often tinged with yellow, sometimes with pink, especially in the center; the flesh is white or pinkish; the gills are thin, crowded, white, then pink, later dark brown, distant from the stem, generally narrowed toward each end; the stem is long, bulbous, stuffed or hollow, whitish, sometimes yellowish below; the ring is membranaceous, sometimes with broad floccose patches on the under side.

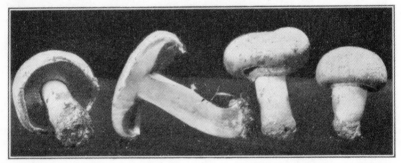

FIGURE 33.—*Agaricus campestris,* the common or cultivated mushroom. (Edible)

AGARICUS CAMPESTRIS. COMMON OR CULTIVATED MUSHROOM. (EDIBLE)

(Fig. 33)

In this species the cap is rounded, convex, when expanded nearly plane, smooth, silky floccose or squamulose, white or light brown, squamules brown, margin incurved; the flesh is white, firm; the gills are white in the very young stage, then pink, soon becoming purplish brown, dark brown, or nearly black, free from the stem, rounded behind, subdeliquescent; the stem is white, subequal, smooth, or nearly so; the veil sometimes remains as fragments on the margin of cap; the ring is frail, sometimes soon disappearing.

The cap is 1½ to 4 inches broad; the stem is 2 to 3 inches long and 4 to 8 lines thick.

This is the most common and best known of all the edible mushrooms. It is a species of high commercial value, lending itself to a very successful and profitable artificial cultivation. It is cosmopolitan in its geographic distribution, being as universally known abroad as in North America. It is cultivated in caves, cellars, and in especially constructed houses; but it also occurs abundantly in the wild state, appearing in pastures, grassy places, golf courses, and richly manured ground. The only danger in collecting it in the wild form is in mistaking an Amanita for an Agaricus; however, this danger may be obviated by waiting until the gills are decidedly pink before collecting the mushrooms.

AGARICUS PLACOMYCES.   FLAT-CAP MUSHROOM.   (EDIBLE)

In this species the cap is thin, at first broadly ovate, convex or expanded and flat in age, whitish, adorned with numerous minute, brown scales, which become crowded in the center, forming a large brown patch; the gills are close, white, then pinkish, finally blackish brown; the veil is broad; the ring is large.   In the early stages, according to Atkinson,[5] a portion of the veil frequently encircles the stipe like a tube, while a part remains still stretched over the gills.   The stem is smooth, stuffed or hollow, bulbous, white or whitish, the bulb often stained with yellow.

The cap is 2 to 4 inches broad; the stem is 3 to 5 inches long and one-fourth to one-half inch thick.

This species frequents hemlock woods, occurring from July to September.

AGARICUS RODMANI.   RODMAN'S AGARIC.   (EDIBLE)

In this species the cap is firm, rounded, convex, then nearly plane, white, becoming subochraceous, smooth or cracked into scales on the disk, margin decurved; the flesh is white; the gills are narrow, close, white, pink or reddish pink, finally blackish brown; the stem is solid, short, whitish, smooth, or slightly mealy, squamulose above the ring; the ring is double, sometimes appearing as two collars with space between.

The cap is 2 to 4 inches broad; the stem is 2 to 3 inches long and 6 to 10 lines thick.

Agaricus rodmani may easily be mistaken for *A. campestris*, but can be distinguished by the thicker, firmer flesh, narrower gills, which are nearly white when young, and the peculiar collar, which appears double.   This species grows on grassy ground, often springing from crevices of unused pavements or between the curbing and the walk.   It is to be found principally from May to July.

AGARICUS SUBRUFESCENS.   (EDIBLE)

In this species the cap is at first deeply hemispherical, becoming convex or broadly expanded, silky, fibrillose, and minutely or obscurely squamulose, whitish, grayish, or dull reddish brown, usually smooth and darker on the disk; the flesh is white, unchangeable; the gills are at first white or whitish, then pinkish, finally blackish brown; the stem is rather long, often somewhat thickened or bulbous at the base, at first stuffed, then hollow, white; the annulus is flocculose or floccose squamose on the lower surface.   Two additional characters that assist in identification are the mycelium, which forms slender branching rootlike. strings, and the almondlike flavor of the flesh.

The cap is 3 to 4 inches broad; the stem is 2½ to 4 inches long.

The plants often grow in large clusters of 20 to 30 or even 40 individuals. They occur in the wild state and have also been reported as a volunteer crop in especially prepared soil.   Specimens collected in the vicinity of Washington, D. C., were found growing near the river on a rocky slope rich in leaf mold.   *Agaricus subrufescens* is considered a very excellent edible species.

STROPHARIA

The genus Stropharia is easily recognized among the purple-spored agarics.   It is distinguished from Agaricus by its usually adnate gills and the continuity of the flesh of the cap and stem.   A ring is always present in young plants but often absent at maturity.   The edibility of species of this genus is a disputed point among mycophagists.

---

[5] ATKINSON, GEORGE F.   STUDIES OF AMERICAN FUNGI, p. 24, 2d ed.   1903.

STROPHARIA SEMIGLOBATA. (POISONOUS)

(Fig. 34)

In *Stropharia semiglobata* the cap is rounded, then hemispherical, thick at center, becoming thin toward the even margin, light yellow, viscid when moist; the gills are broad, adnate, unequal, when young light brown, later purplish brown or blackish; the stem is slender, hollow, even or slightly bulbous,

FIGURE 34.—*Stropharia semiglobata.* (Poisonous)

smooth, yellowish, but paler at apex, where striate markings from the gills may be present, viscid; the ring is viscous, incomplete, and formed by the remains of the glutinous veil which soon disappears.

FIGURE 35.—*Hypholoma appendiculatum.* (Edible.)   (From G. F. Atkinson)

The cap is 1 to 1½ inches broad; the stem is 2 to 3 inches long and 2 to 3 lines thick.

This species is remarkable for the uniformly hemispherical cap. It occurs commonly on dung or in well-manured ground. It is not to be recognized as an edible species.

HYPHOLOMA

The genus Hypholoma belongs to the purple-brown-spored group, but differs from Agaricus and Stropharia in the character of the veil, which persists as fragments or a silky border on the margin of the pileus.   In some species the latter is firm and fleshy, in others fragile.   The margin of the pileus is at first incurved.   The stem is fleshy and like Stropharia continuous with the substance of the cap. Species of the genus Hypholoma generally occur in clusters or clumps at the base of dead stumps, logs, or decayed wood under the ground.

HYPHOLOMA APPENDICULATUM.   (EDIBLE)
(Fig. 35)

In this species the cap is rather thin, ovate, then expanded until somewhat flattened, dark brown when damp, tawny when dry, slightly wrinkled and atomate; the flesh is white; the gills are crowded, somewhat adnate, white, at length purplish brown; the stem is white, hollow, equal, smooth, pruinose at the apex; the veil is white, delicate, attached to the margin of the cap for a short time, soon disappearing.

The cap is 2 to 3 inches broad; the stem is 2 to 3 inches long and 2 to 3 lines thick.

Specimens of this species may be collected in the late spring, in summer, and frequently in the early fall.   The plants are fragile and hygrophanous, scattered, clustered, or densely tufted.   They grow on rotten logs, stumps, or sometimes on the ground, arising mostly from rotten wood beneath the surface.

This species is tender and possesses excellent esculent qualities.   Drying and preserving for winter use have been recommended, as the flavor is retained to a remarkable degree.

FIGURE 36.—*Hypholoma sublateritium.*   (Suspected.)   (From G. F. Atkinson)

HYPHOLOMA SUBLATERITIUM.   BRICK-TOP.   (SUSPECTED)
(Fig. 36)

In this species the cap is conical, becoming almost plane, fleshy, firm, smooth, but with fine, silky fibers, brick red, sometimes tawny, margin of lighter color; the flesh is white or yellowish; the gills are narrow, crowded, adnate, sometimes decurrent by a tooth, creamy when young, purplish olivaceous, sometimes with a sooty tinge when mature; the stem is firm, stuffed, attenuated downward, smooth or fibrillose, scaly, light yellowish, rust colored below; the veil is at first white, becoming dark, and may for a time adhere to the margin of the cap.

The cap is 2 to 3 inches broad; the stem is 3 to 4 inches long and 3 to 5 lines thick.

This species appears very abundantly in the fall, producing large clusters around rotten stumps or decayed prostrate logs. The European form of this plant is reported as bitter and regarded as poisonous. The American form has been frequently eaten, although it has little to recommend it as a delicacy. Catchup has been made from it, but the success of the experiment was doubtless due more to the addition of condiments than to the flavor of the mushrooms.

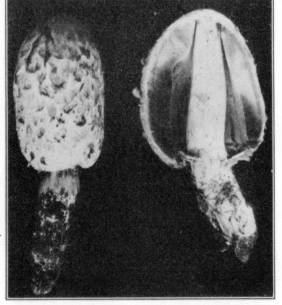

FIGURE 37.—*Coprinus comatus.*   (Edible)

HYPHOLOMA PERPLEXUM.
PERPLEXING HYPHOLOMA

In this species the cap is convex, expanding to nearly plane, sometimes umbonate, smooth, reddish, or brownish red, margin yellowish; the flesh is white or whitish; the gills are thin, close rounded at inner extremity, first pale yellow then greenish, later purplish brown; the stem is equal, hollow, fibrillose, yellowish above, reddish-brown below.

The cap is 1 to 3 inches broad; the stem is 2 to 3 inches long and 2 to 4 lines thick.

Hypholoma sublateritium and *H. perplexum* are very closely related, and by some authorities the latter is regarded as only a variety of *H. sublateritium*, while certain mycologists consider the two species identical. Peck [6] states that *H. perplexum* may be distinguished by its smaller size, more hollow stem, the yellowish-greenish and purplish tints of the gills, and the absence of a bitter flavor. Like *H. sublateritium*, this species occurs abundantly in the fall about stumps or logs, often continuing until freezing weather. The plants grow in clusters and the caps are frequently discolored by the falling spores.

COPRINUS

The genus Coprinus is easily recognized by the black spores and the close gills, which at maturity dissolve into an inky fluid. The stem is hollow, smooth or fibrillose. The volva and ring are not generic characters, but are sometimes present. The plants are more or less fragile and occur on richly manured ground, on dung, or on rotten tree trunks. The genus contains species of excellent flavor and delicate consistency.

COPRINUS COMATUS.   SHAGGY MANE.   (EDIBLE)

(Fig. 37)

In this species the cap is oblong, bell-shaped, not fully expanding, fleshy at center, moist, cuticle separating into scales that are sometime white, sometimes

[6] PECK, CHARLES II.   Op. cit.

yellowish or darker, and show the white flesh beneath, splitting from the margin along the lines of the gills; the gills are broad, crowded, free, white, soon becoming pink or salmon colored and changing to purplish black just previous to deliquescence; the stem is brittle, smooth or fibrillose, hollow, thick, attenuated upward, sometimes slightly bulbous at base, easily separating from the cap; the ring is thin, movable.

The cap is usually 1½ to 3 inches long; the stem is 2 to 4 inches long and 4 to 6 lines thick.

This species has a wide geographic distribution and is universally enjoyed by mycophagists. The fungus is very attractive when young, often white, again showing gray, tawny, or pinkish tints. It appears in the spring and fall, sometimes solitary, sometimes in groups, on lawns, in rich soil, or in gardens.

COPRINUS ATRAMENTARI-
US. INKY CAP. (EDIBLE)

(Fig. 38)

In this mushroom the cap is ovate, slightly expanding, silvery to dark gray or brownish, smooth, silky or with small scales, especially at the center, often plicate and lobed with notched margin; the gills are broad, ventricose, crowded, free, white, soon changing to pinkish gray, then becoming black and deliquescent; the stem is smooth, shining, whitish, hollow, attenuated upward, readily separating from the cap; the ring is near the base of stem, evanescent.

FIGURE 38.—*Coprinus atramentarius* (smooth form). (Edible)

The cap is 1½ to 4 inches broad; the stem is 2 to 4 inches long and 4 to 7 lines thick.

This species appears from spring to autumn, particularly after rains. It grows singly or in dense clusters on rich ground, lawns, gardens, or waste places. It has long been esteemed as an edible species. *Coprinus atramentarius* differs from *C. comatus* in the more or less smooth, oval cap and the imperfect, basal, evanescent ring.

COPRINUS MICACEUS.   MICA INKY CAP.   (EDIBLE)

In this species the cap is ovate, bell-shaped, light tan to brown, darker when moist or old, often glistening from minute, micalike particles, margin closely striate, splitting, and revolute; the gills are narrow, crowded, white, then pink before becoming black; stem is slender, white, hollow, fragile, often twisted.

The cap is 1 to 2 inches broad; the stem is 2 to 4 inches long and 2 to 3 lines thick.

This glistening little species occurs very commonly at the base of trees or springing from dead roots along pavements, or more uncommonly on prostrate logs in shady woods. The plants appear in great profusion in the spring and early summer, and more sparingly during the fall. *Coprinus micaceus* is a very delicious mushroom and lends itself to various methods of preparation.

PSATHYRELLA

The species comprising the genus Psathyrella are all fragile, having thin membranaceous, striate caps. When young the margin of the cap lies against the stem, but never extends beyond the gills.

PSATHYRELLA DISSEMINATA.   (EDIBLE)

The cap is thin, oval to bell-shaped, yellowish, gray or grayish brown, minutely scaly, becoming smooth, sulcate or plicate, margin entire; the gills are broad, adnate, white, then gray, later black; the stem is hollow, slender, fragile.

The cap is about one-half inch broad; the stem is 1 to 1½ inches long and 1 to 1½ lines thick.

This is a delicate little species, appearing in densely cespitose clusters on decaying wood or about old roots of trees. It occurs from May until frost, often intermittently from the same center This species is edible, but has too little substance to render it a popular article of diet.

FIGURE 39.—*Panaeolus retirugis*

PANAEOLUS

In the genus Panaeolus the cap is slightly fleshy and the margin nonstriate, always extending beyond the gills, which are gray and mottled from the falling of the black spores. The stem is without a ring and polished. The two nearest related genera are Psathyrella and Coprinus. Panaeolus is distinguished from Psathyrella by the nonstriate margin of the cap and from Coprinus by the nondeliquescent gills.

PANAEOLUS RETIRUGIS. WRINKLED PANAEOLUS

(Fig. 39)

The cap is ovate, conic, slightly expanding, almost hemispherical, cream to tan colored, becoming grayish and dark smoky, viscid in wet weather, irregularly marked with anastomosing wrinkles; remnants of veil, which is prominent and firm in young plants, adhering as fragments on the margin of the mature caps; the gills are rather broad, ascending, adnexed, grayish to violet black; the stem is color of cap, darker in lower part, hollow, smooth, granulate, may be slightly bulbous.

The cap is three-fourths to 1½ inches broad; the stem is 2 to 4 inches long and 2 to 3 lines thick.

This species is to be found on dung or on richly manured lawns. While it is not generally considered poisonous it is wise not to use it as food, as it might be confused with other species of the genus that are poisonous.

POLYPORACEAE (PORE FUNGI)

In the Polyporaceae or pore fungi are found the large woody forms that are so often seen on forest and ornamental trees and that cause most of the serious diseases of timber and forest trees. As a class they are difficult to control, because the mycelium lives in the wood, rendering the use of fungicides impracticable. The conspicuous shelving, woody growths seen on the branches and trunks of trees are the fruiting bodies of the fungi. These may be removed, but the mycelium will remain to continue the work of destruction.

In Polyporaceae the spores are produced in minute pores or tubes (fig. 1, B), instead of on gills as in Agaricaceae, a character suggestive of the name polypores, meaning many pores. The pores are developed on the lower surface of the fruiting body and in many species may be seen without the aid of a lens. The tubes or pores vary greatly in size and shape, being long or short, round or angular, or compressed. In some genera the hymenium is wrinkled and the pores are reduced to mere pits. Great variation is also to be observed in the consistency of the fruiting body; it may be woody, fleshy, coriaceous, or subgelatinous. The key that follows will aid in distinguishing the genera of Polyporaceae discussed in this circular.

KEY TO POLYPORACEAE

Hymenophore normally pileate, sometimes with resupinate forms.
    Tubes poroid:
        Stratum of tubes separable from the hymenophore
          and from each other—   *Genus*
            Cap fleshy, tubes crowded_____ FISTULINA.
        Stratum of tubes separable from the hymenophore,
          stem central—
            Cap smooth _____ BOLETUS.
            Cap with large scales_____ STROBILOMYCES
        Stratum of tubes distinct from the hymenophore, but
          not separable from it—
            Tubes in several layers, woody, perennial_____ FOMES.
            Tubes not stratose—
                Cap thick_____ POLYPORUS.
                Cap thin_____ POLYSTICTUS.
    Tubes labyrinthiform, sinuous—
        Hymenophore sessile, corky_____ DAEDALEA.
Hymenophore reflexed, resupinate or amorphous, subgelatinous,
    hymenium plicate or rugose porous_____ MERULIUS.

FISTULINA

In the genus Fistulina the stem is lateral or very short, the fruiting body growing horizontally from trunks of living trees or stumps of recently cut trees. It is distinguished from species of Polyporus by

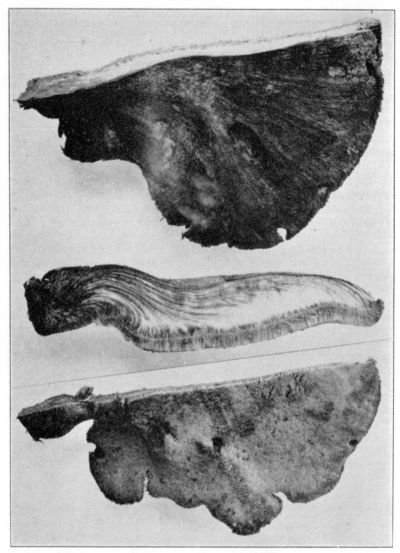

FIGURE 40.—*Fistulina hepatica.* (Edible)

the tubes, which are separate from one another and closed at the mouth when young.

FISTULINA HEPATICA. BEEFSTEAK FUNGUS. (EDIBLE)

(Fig. 40)

Specimens of this species are always shelving and may be sessile or stipitate. The caps are tongue-shaped, the margin is entire, wavy or scalloped, blood red, and at maturity marked with more or less radiating lines. The flesh is red, thick, soft, juicy, and traversed by tenacious fibers. The tubes are at first short and yellowish, becoming elongated and discolored in age.

The cap is 3½ to 8 inches broad, reported as attaining in England a weight of 30 pounds.

This fungus is variously known as the beefsteak fungus, beef tongue, oak tongue, or chestnut tongue. It grows from decaying crevices of certain deciduous trees, such as oak and chestnut, but preferably the chestnut. The beefsteak fungus is widely distributed and has an international reputation for its edibility.

BOLETUS

In general appearance, namely, the pileate and stipitate character of the plants, the species of the genus Boletus resemble members of the Agaricaceae. The important difference is the fact that in species of Boletus the spores, instead of being developed on gills, are borne in numerous small tubes, which are closely crowded but easily separable from one another and from the hymenophore.

Most of the plants of this genus are terrestrial, but occasionally they are to be found growing on wood. Some species are edible and considered exceedingly good, while others are extremely dangerous. The phenomenon of changing color on exposure to air exhibited by certain species is not a character peculiar to either poisonous or edible varieties.

KEY TO SPECIES OF BOLETUS

Surface of hymenium yellow, orange, or greenish.
    Ring present; cap distinctly viscid when moist; stem
        granular-dotted above the ring_____ *B. luteus.*
    Ring absent:
        Stem more or less dotted with granules; pileus distinctly viscid when moist—
            Stem long and distinctly granular-dotted_____ *B. granulatus.*
            Stem short and indistinctly granular-dotted_____ *B. brevipes.*
        Stem not dotted with granules, but reticulate with a
        network of lines, pruinose, or fibrous-striate—
            Stem reticulate—
                Tube mouths eventually bright red to orange;
                    surface of cap becoming whitish_____ *B. satanas.*
                Tube mouths flesh color; cap brownish tawny;
                    flesh bitter to the taste_____ *B. felleus.*
                Tube mouths creamy white then greenish_____ *B. edulis.*
            Stem not reticulate—
                Pileus and stem dark red and pruinose; tubes
                    bright yellow changing to blue when
                    wounded_____ *B. bicolor.*
                Pileus darkish fuscous red, surface areolate
                  cracked, the interstices red; stem fibrous-
                  striate; tubes bright yellow then greenish
                  blue_____ *B. chrysenteron.*
                Pileus bay brown; stem brown; pruinate;
                  tubes creamy citron, turning bluish green
                  when touched_____ *B. badius.*

BOLETUS LUTEUS.   (EDIBLE)

The cap is convex, becoming nearly plane, viscid or glutinous when moist, dull yellowish to reddish brown, sometimes streaked or spotted; the flesh is whitish or dull yellowish; the tubes are adnate, minute, yellow becoming darker with age; the stem is stout, pale yellowish, brownish or reddish, dotted above the annulus; the annulus is variable, sometimes persisting as a narrow ring and again appearing as a broad collar.

The cap is 3 to 4 inches broad; the stem is 2½ to 3 inches high.

This is an excellent edible species of wide geographic distribution, occurring commonly in pine woods.

A very similar species is *Boletus subluteus*, which is ornamented with dots both above and below the annulus. This fungus also is considered edible.

BOLETUS GRANULATUS

The cap is convex or nearly plane, color variable, when moist viscid and reddish brown, paler and yellowish when dry; viscid or glutinous; the flesh is pale yellow; the tubes are short, adnate, yellowish, mouths granulated; the stem is pale yellowish, dotted above.

A nearly related species, *Boletus brevipes*, is distinguished from *B. granulatus* by a shorter stem and the absence or indistinctness of granulations on the mouths of the tubes and stem.

Figure 41.—*Boletus felleus* (form with nonreticulate stem)

BOLETUS FELLEUS. BITTER BOLETUS

(Fig. 41)

The cap is convex or nearly plane, firm, becoming soft, color variable, pale yellowish, grayish brown, reddish brown, or chestnut; the flesh is white, often changing to flesh color when wounded, and of bitter taste; the tubes are adnate, long, depressed around the stem, mouths angular, white, becoming tinged with flesh color; the stem is similar in color to the cap, but paler, variable, long or short, equal or tapering upward, sometimes bulbous, reticulated above.

The cap is 3 to 4 inches broad; the stem is 2 to 3 inches long.

This is a common and widely distributed species. It is exceedingly conspicuous on account of its color, size, and solidity; though not poisonous, it is very bitter.

A variety, *Boletus felleus obesus*, attains a size of about a foot in diameter and has coarse reticulations on the stem.

BOLETUS CHRYSENTERON

The cap is convex or plane, brown or brick red, more or less cracked, subtomentose; the flesh is yellow, red immediately beneath the cuticle, changing to slight blue where wounded; the tubes are subadnate, yellow then greenish, large, angular; the stem is fibrous, striate, equal, red or yellowish.

The cap is 1 to 3 inches broad; the stem is 1 to 3 inches long.

Authors differ concerning the edibility of this species; consequently extreme caution should be used to avoid collecting it for *Boletus bicolor,* which is edible.

BOLETUS EDULIS.   EDIBLE BOLETUS.   (EDIBLE)

(Fig. 42)

The cap is convex to expanded, smooth, firm when young, becoming soft in age, the color varying from grayish red to brownish red, generally paler on the margin; the flesh is white or yellowish, sometimes reddish beneath the cuticle; the tubes are convex, nearly free, long, minute, white, then yellow, and greenish; the stem is variable in length, straight or flexuous, equal or bulbous, more or less reticulated, whitish, pallid, or brownish.

The cap is 4 to 6 inches broad; the stem is 2 to 6 inches long.

This is a species of frequent occurrence and the one of this genus most commonly eaten.

BOLETUS BICOLOR
(EDIBLE)

The cap is convex, glabrous, pruinose, dark red, paler in age and sometimes spotted with yellow, firm; the flesh is yellow, sometimes changing to blue where wounded; the tubes are nearly plane, adnate, bright yellow, changing to blue where wounded, mouths small angular or subrotund; the stem is subequal, solid, red.

FIGURE 42.—*Boletus edulis.*   (Edible)

The cap is 2 to 4 inches broad; the stem is 1 to 3 inches long.

This is a very attractive little species, occurring quite commonly in Virginia and Maryland in the woods and on lawns in shady places. It is considered one of the best edible species.

STROBILOMYCES

The genus Strobilomyces closely resembles Boletus, but it may be distinguished by the less easily separable tubes and extremely scaly cap and stem.

STROBILOMYCES STROBILACEUS.   PORE CONE

(Fig. 43)

The cap is hemispherical or convex, shaggy from numerous coarse, blackish scales, margin more or less appendiculate from the scales and fragments of the veil, which covers the tubes in the young plant; the flesh is at first whitish, changing to reddish, then blackish where wounded; the tubes are adnate, at first whitish, becoming blackish with age, mouths large, angular, changing color like the flesh; the stem is even or tapering above, sulcate at the top, scaly, colored like the cap.

The cap is 2 to 4 inches broad; the stem is 3 to 5 inches long and 4 to 10 lines thick.

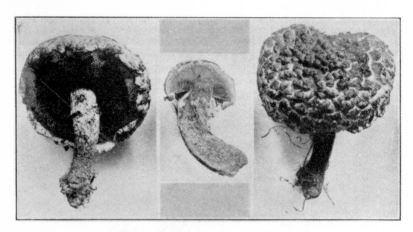

FIGURE 43.—*Strobilomyces strobilaceus*

This conspicuous but unattractive plant occurs commonly in woods and along roadsides, singly, in small groups, or occasionally cespitose, from early summer until autumn.

FOMES

The genus Fomes is distinguished among the Polyporaceae by the hard, woody character of the species. The hymenophore is bracket shaped; the tubes are much elongated and stratified, one stratum developing annually. Fomes contains no edible varieties, but comprises many serious tree-destroying species.

FOMES APPLANATUS.   SHELF FOMES

In *Fomes applanatus* the cap or fruiting body is smooth, cinnamon brown, becoming hoary, horizontal, flattened, shelflike, concentrically zoned, semicircular, broadly attached, margin thickened, first white, later becoming brown; the hymenium is flat, pores small, mouths white, changing to brown when bruised; internal structure of fibrous-spongy texture, brown in color.

The cap is 2½ to 8 inches broad and 2 inches or more thick.

This species is perennial and of common occurrence on various deciduous trees.

FOMES LUCIDUS.   LACQUERED FOMES

In *Fomes lucidus* the cap is horizontal, irregularly kidney-shaped, blood red, surface uneven, coarsely grooved, polished, corky, light in weight; the stem is lateral, length variable, polished, same color as the cap; the tubes are small, white, then tan.

The cap is 2 to 6 inches broad.

This fungus is of wide distribution and of common occurrence, appearing on logs and trunks. It is easily recognized by the brittle varnished crust of the cap and stem.

POLYPORUS

Species belonging to the genus Polyporus present considerable variation in stem, form, and texture. The stem may be central, excentric, or absent; the hymenophore circular, reniform, or hoof shaped, azonate or grooved; and the substance fleshy, soft, corky, or woody. This genus is distinguished from Polystictus by the thicker cap and from Fomes by the nonstratose tubes.

Species of this genus are widely distributed, and representatives may be found from the extreme North to the Tropics. Polyporus contains a few edible species and many wound parasites, species injurious to economic and ornamental trees. Wound parasites are fungi that gain entrance to the interior of a tree or host through some unprotected surface resulting from injury by lightning, insect attack, injudicious pruning, or some other agency.

POLYPORUS BETULINUS. BIRCH POLYPORUS

In the birch polypore the hymenophore is tough and fleshy, then corky, hoof shaped, umbonate at point of attachment, margin thickened, obtuse incurved, white when young, later light to dark mottled gray, zoneless, smooth; the pores are minute, short, unequal, whitish.

The fungus is of common occurrence on birch trees, measuring from 3 to 8 inches or more in width. When young it is considered edible, but is tough and possesses a rather strong flavor. It is often used as material for outdoor sketching, for which purpose it is very well adapted.

POLYPORUS FRONDOSUS

This species occurs in large tufts, which measure 6 inches to over a foot in breadth. The caps are very numerous, crowded and overlapping, 1 to 2 inches in diameter, irregular in shape, curved, repand, lobed or cleft, brown or sooty gray; the stems are indefinite, branching or confluent; the pores are very small, white.

This is a very common plant, growing about stumps, roots, and trunks. It is edible and tender when young, but soon becomes tough.

POLYPORUS SULPHUREUS. SULPHUR POLYPORUS

This is a very conspicuous fungus on account of its large clusters and the characteristic sulphur-yellow color. The caps are fleshy, spongy, attached laterally, very much imbricated, more or less fan shaped, smooth, even when young, later ridged and furrowed; margin at first thick and blunt, becoming thinner; the pores are very small, plane and sulphur yellow.

Polyporus sulphureus occurs abundantly and is edible, though of doubtful value. It is of interest as a wound parasite on various trees, gaining entrance to the interior of a tree through an exposed surface and finally causing the death of the host. This is a very striking plant on account of the bright sulphur-yellow color, which quickly attracts the attention of the collector.

POLYSTICTUS

Species of the genus Polystictus may be differentiated from those of Polyporus because of being thinner with caps more pliant. None are to be especially recommended for table purposes, but by their abundance and attractiveness they force themselves upon the attention of the amateur or nature student. The species described here are all sessile and shelving.

POLYSTICTUS CINNABARINUS

The specific name of this plant is derived from its bright cinnabar color. The fungus is shelving, pliant, and rather thicker than the following species. It grows on dead logs or dead branches of various trees.

The cap is 1 to 3 inches in width.

This fungus has a very wide geographic range and is quickly located by its bright and beautiful color.

POLYSTICTUS PERGAMENUS

This fungus is thin and very pliant when fresh, somewhat tomentose, with indistinct, longitudinal color zones. The tubes are violet or purplish, but the plants are easily weathered, and the tubes become lacerated, resembling Irpex, a genus possessing teeth instead of tubes.

The cap is 1 to 1½ inches in width.

This is one of the most common Polypores and is to be found on various trees.

POLYSTICTUS VERSICOLOR

Polystictus versicolor is easily distinguished by the concentric bands of different colors, mostly bay or black but occasionally with a narrow zone of orange, which mark the cap. The tubes are white, and the margin is thin, sterile, and entire. The plants grow densely imbricated and are to be found abundantly on dead stumps or trunks of many varieties of trees.

The cap is three-fourths to 1½ inches in width.

DAEDALEA

The plants belonging to the genus Daedalea are sessile, dry, and corky. The species are exceedingly interesting on account of the hymenophore, which shows intermediate stages between the gill and pore fungi. The pores are typically sinuous and labyrinthiform, but often the thick platelike developments resemble gills more than pores. Several species are of common occurrence, but all are tough and corky and none are reported edible.

DAEDALEA QUERCINA

In this species the cap is shelflike, dimidiate, triangular in cross section, corky, rigid, smooth or nearly so, wrinkled, grayish to light brownish, margin usually thin, pallid; the pores are wavy, some gill-like.

The cap is 2 to 4½ inches or more in width.

This species occurs on oak (Quercus) stumps and trunks, and because of its habit of growing on this host it was named *Daedalea quercina.*

MERULIUS

The species of the genus Merulius are resupinate and subgelatinous. The hymenium is wrinkled or foldlike, and the pores are very shallow.

Species of Merulius are very destructive in dwellings constructed wholly or in part of timber. It is probably the most destructive timber rot, as it affects both softwoods and hardwoods. Attacks by these fungi are common where the light and ventilation are poor, as in cellars, basements, and similar places.

MERULIUS LACRYMANS. WEEPING MERULIUS

In *Merulius lacrymans* the fruiting body is flat, prostrate, soft, and characterized by watery exudations. It is at first white, then red, later changing to yellowish brown. This is one of the most common species that attack timber, rendering it spongy, watery, and unfit for building purposes. The mycelium may develop as long strands, or it may form large sheets which peel off readily.

HYDNACEAE (TOOTH FUNGI)

In the family Hydnaceae the plants are stipitate, bracket shaped or resupinate, fleshy, corky, leathery, or woody. In Hydnum, the most highly developed genus of this family, the hymenium is distinctly toothlike, but there are many intermediate gradations, from scattered granules or small hemispherical prominences to toothlike developments. In all having teeth, the processes are directed downward.

KEY TO HYDNACEAE

Hymenium of distinct, awl-shaped teeth or spines, resupinate
  or with central stem: *Genus*
    Plants fleshy_____ HYDNUM.
    Plants woody_____ ECHINODONTIUM.
Hymenium with teeth united (connected at the base by slightly
  raised folds), plants leathery, teeth not so acute as in
  Hydnum_____ IRPEX.
Hymenium with coarse, blunt tubercles, subcylindrical, re-
  supinate_____ RADULUM.

HYDNUM

The species of the genus Hydnum vary greatly as to form, consistency, and manner of growth. Certain forms possess well-defined cap and stem, some are bracket shaped or shelving, and still others are resupinate. The teeth are pointed and free from each other at the base. In consistency, species of Hydnum range from soft fleshy to tough. Many are terrestrial in habit, while others grow on living or dead trees.

HYDNUM CORALLOIDES. CORAL HYDNUM. (EDIBLE)

This species is easily recognized by the long, interlacing, tapering branches, which are of two kinds: The primary, which are nearly sterile; and the secondary, which are fertile and chiefly bear the slender terete teeth. The substance is fleshy, brittle to somewhat tough. *Hydnum coralloides* is one of the most graceful and beautiful species of fungi, and its white, corallike tufts measure from 6 to 18 inches across. It grows on decaying prostrate or standing timber and is found from August until frost. It is edible, but not very abundant or common.

HYDNUM ERINACEUS. SATYR'S BEARD. (EDIBLE)

(Fig. 44)

Hydnum erinaceus forms pendulous tufts from 2 to 10 inches across. The point of attachment is small and the mass generally projects horizontally from the substratum. The tufts are white, changing to yellowish brown in drying. The individual teeth are crowded, slender, terete, tapering, acute, 1 to 2½ inches long. This species is quite conspicuous, growing from crotches or wounds of trees—beech, oak, locust, etc. Growth from the same source may appear year after year.

CLAVARIACEAE (CORAL FUNGI)

The common name of the coral fungi was given them on account of their resemblance to coral. They are erect, club-shaped, simple, or branched and vary in size from slender clubs to large, many-branched masses. In many species the color is very beautiful and may be lavender, pink, orange, cream, or white. Certain members of this family are edible, but as the species are difficult to recognize and as cases of poisoning have been reported, it is safer to let all coral fungi alone.

PHALLACEAE (STINKHORN FUNGI)

Most of the species belonging to the family Phallaceae are characterized by a disagreeable odor. The plants grow below the surface of the ground or on decayed stumps. The mycelium or vegetative part forms coarse, ropelike strands from which arises the fruit body. which in its early stages is commonly known as an " egg " because of its form. The outer part of the egg forms the volva and consists of outer and inner membranes, between which is a gelatinous substance.

FIGURE 44.—*Hydnum erinaceus.* (Edible)

The central portion of the egg is occupied by a tubular receptacle or part bearing the gleba, the spore-bearing part. The receptacle, elongates rapidly and at maturity ruptures the volva, thus exposing the spore-bearing mass. Species of this family have highly developed characters, such as color, taste, and odor, which, by attracting insects, insure the dissemination of the spores. The following fungi are two very common examples of this family:

ITHYPHALLUS IMPUDICUS. STINKHORN FUNGUS

(Fig. 45)

In this fungus the volva is globose or ovoid, white or pinkish, and divides into two or three parts as the plant develops. The cap is conic to campanulate, the surface reticulate pitted, the apex smooth, and the stalk cylindric-fusiform, hollow, and widely perforate at the apex.

This is a very common species and is found about dead stumps, fence corners, and yards, or under walks or platforms. Its presence is readily detected by the strong, disagreeable odor which is emitted at maturity.

MUTINUS

In the genus Mutinus the receptacle or stalk is cellular or spongy, simple, elongated, cylindric tapering, with the gleba-bearing portion at the apex. The species of Mutinus are very similar in general form and color.

MUTINUS CANINUS.   DOG STINKHORN

In this plant the stipe is hollow, perforate or imperforate, fusiform, white or reddish; spore-bearing portion of flesh is colored, sharply defined, cellular structure not uniform; e. g., the cells or minute chambers composing the stem are larger than those of the gleba-bearing portion.

This species is common and appears in summer and autumn, occurring on the ground in woods. Its bright red c o l o r is conspicuous among the greens and browns of the woods as well as its odor, which though disagreeable is n o t a s offensive a s *Ithyphallus impudicus.*

LYCOPERDACEAE (PUFFBALLS)

The Lycoperdaceae include the puffballs and earth stars. They are more or less ball s h a p e d, sometimes with a thickened base, sessile or indefinitely stipitate and when mature filled with a dusty mass consisting of spores and fine cobwebby filaments known as capillitium. In addition to the puffball type t h i s family contains some

FIGURE 45.—*Ithyphallus impudicus*

very queer and strange fungi, which present great variation in shape, structure, and color.

LYCOPERDON

Species of the genus Lycoperdon are small puffballs with a somewhat thickened base and fibrous rooting mycelium. The covering or peridium consists of two layers. The outer layer, the cortex, breaks up into small, soft scales, spines, warts, or granules, which may soon disappear; the inner, the true peridium, is smooth, thin, and membranaceous, and opens by an apical mouth. When young the interior of the plant is white, soft, and firm; as it matures it changes to yellow and finally forms a purplish or olivaceous brown, dusty mass.

All species of this genus are considered edible if collected while the interior is firm and white; the flavor, however, is inferior to that of large puffballs. Species of Lycoperdon are commonly found on the ground or on old stumps or logs, and are generally clustered, appearing in the summer and autumn.

LYCOPERDON PYRIFORME.   PEAR-SHAPED PUFFBALL.   (EDIBLE)

(Fig. 46)

In this species the plants are obovate, pear-shaped or subglobose, dingy white or brown; the cortex consists of minute, persistent warts or scales, with the inner coat smooth; they are sessile or with a short stemlike base and with white rootlike fibers; columellæ are present; capillitium and spores

FIGURE 46.—*Lycoperdon pyriforme.*   (Edible)

are greenish, yellow, then olivaceous. The plants are 1 to 2 inches in height and about 1 inch in diameter.

This is a very common species, sometimes called the stump puffball, appearing in dense clusters on rotten stumps or logs.

CALVATIA

The genus Calvatia contains puffballs of the largest size. It differs from Lycoperdon in the absence of an apical mouth and a regular method of dehiscence. The plants are terrestrial, globose, or top-shaped, usually with a thick, cordlike, rooting mycelium. The cortex is thin and smooth or covered with minute squamules.

The most delicious species of puffballs belong to this genus, but as is the case with all fungi of this class they must be eaten while the interior is perfectly white. If old they are unpalatable and indigestible.

CALVATIA CYATHIFORMIS.   CUP PUFFBALL.   (EDIBLE)

In this species the plant is globose or turbinate and depressed above, with a thick, somewhat stemlike base and cordlike root; the cortex is whitish gray or brown, sometimes with a pinkish-purple tinge, thin, fragile, areolate in the upper part, which, after maturity, soon breaks up and falls away, leaving a cup-shaped base with a ragged margin attached to the ground; the capillitium and spores are at first violet, becoming dark purple brown. The plant is 3 to 6 inches in diameter.

This species is common on open grassy ground in pastures, fields, and lawns. It is edible and of fine flavor.

CALVATIA GIGANTEA.   GIANT PUFFBALL.   (EDIBLE)

(Fig. 47)

The giant puffball is globose or obovoid in shape, nearly sessile, plicate at the base, with cordlike mycelial strands. The cortex is at first white and smooth, becoming yellowish or brown, sometimes slightly roughened by minute warts or cracking in areas; the inner peridium is thin and fragile; the capillitium and spores are yellowish green to dingy olive when mature.

FIGURE 47.—*Calvatia gigantea.*   (Edible)

Individuals of this species often attain an enormous size, the specimen shown in Figure 47 measuring 5 feet 1 inch in circumference. The usual size, however, varies from 10 to 20 inches in diameter.

This is an excellent edible species of wide geographic range, growing very abundantly on lawns, pastures, and meadows.

GEASTER (EARTH STARS)

In the genus Geaster the peridium consists of three persistent coats. The two outer coats generally adhere and form the thick, fleshy-coriaceous layer (exoperidium), which at maturity splits from the apex into several segments; the inner coat is more or less parchmentlike, either sessile or short stalked, and opens by an apical mouth. The spores are usually dark brown and mixed with capillitium.

The distinctive character of this genus is the stellate manner of dehiscence, or breaking, of the two outer layers. The segments thus formed may be spreading, inrolled, incurved, or arched. Figure 48 shows a form of the latter type in which the two layers of the exoperidium separate, the outer remaining as a segmented basal cup while the inner layer becomes arched and causes the elevation of the endoperidium.

GEASTER HYGROMETRICUS. BAROMETER EARTH STAR

In this species the peridium is depressed globose; the exoperidium splitting at the apex divides into a variable number of strongly hygroscopic segments, which are rigidly inrolled when dry and expanded when moist; the endoperidium is whitish gray or brown, thin, membranaceous, with a small irregular mouth.

The inner peridium is three-fourths to 1 inch in diameter. The segments are 6 to 20 in number and are 2 to 3 inches in diameter when expanded.

FIGURE 48.—*Geaster radicans.* (From C. G. Lloyd)

Geaster hygrometricus is the species most frequently collected. It is common in woods, sandy locations, or partly cleared land. The peculiarity of this species is the hygroscopic nature of the exoperidium, the segments of which in dry weather are strongly recurved and in wet weather expand. This process may occur repeatedly, depending on weather conditions, and has given rise to the common name for this species, the poor man's weatherglass."

ASCOMYCETES (SAC FUNGI)

The group of fungi known as Ascomycetes comprise a very large number of species remarkable for great variation in form, structure, color, size, and habit. In the species considered so far the spores have been borne externally on a more or less club-shaped body known as the basidium, generally four spores to a basidium. In the Ascomycetes the spores are produced in very small sacs or asci, the term Ascomycete being derived from two Greek words meaning sac fungi. There are generally 8 spores or some multiple of 8— though occasionally 4—in an ascus. The spores are very minute, and without the aid of a microscope they appear as a fine powder.

Many of the species of Ascomycetes are highly parasitic and cause many serious diseases of agricultural crops, while a few are edible and highly regarded as articles of food, as, for example, truffles and morels. While certain species of truffles are to be found in the United States, they are not very common or well known. Morels, on the contrary, have a wider geographic distribution and being terrestrial instead of subterranean like truffles are more conspicuous and better known.

MORCHELLA, MOREL

The morels, belonging to the genus Morchella, are very easily distinguished by the prominently ridged and pitted cap, which is hollow and continuous with the cavity of the stem to which it is adnate throughout its length. The plants are stipitate, waxy, and brittle in consistency, and the caps are conic or cylindric to ovate in shape.

From early historic times the morels have been considered among the choicest edible fungi.

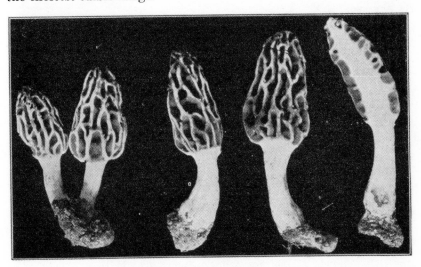

FIGURE 49.—*Morchella esculenta.* (Edible)

MORCHELLA ESCULENTA.   MOREL.   (EDIBLE)

(Fig. 49)

The species of most common occurrence is *Morchella esculenta*, the common morel, or, as it is sometimes known, the sponge mushroom. The plants are from 2 to 4 inches high and about 1½ to 2 inches broad; the cap is ovate or oblong, deeply pitted, dingy yellow or tawny; the stem is 1 to 2 inches long, stout, generally hollow, whitish. This species is widely distributed and occurs abundantly on the ground, particularly along banks of streams or in sandy localities.

Considerable variation in shape may be observed among individual specimens of a single collection. The caps may vary from conical to ovate. Certain authorities consider this a specific difference and others a variety.

COLLATERAL READING

As indicated in the introduction of this circular, only a few of the more common mushrooms that appear in our fields and forests are here discussed. To obtain more complete information on the hundreds of other species the student may encounter, reference should be made to one or more of the various mushroom manuals or monographic works on the subject that have appeared in this country. A selected list of these follows. Though many of these are no longer in print, most of them can be consulted in libraries or in some instances purchased in second-hand book stores. Several of the more recent works are still available from the publishers.

(1) ATKINSON, G. F.
    1911. MUSHROOMS, EDIBLE, POISONOUS, ETC. Ed. 3, 323 pp., illus. New York.
(2) CHRISTENSEN, C. M.
    1943. COMMON EDIBLE MUSHROOMS. 124 pp., illus. Minneapolis, Minn.
(3) COKER, W. C.
    1923. THE CLAVARIAS OF THE UNITED STATES AND CANADA. 209 pp., illus. Chapel Hill, N. C.
(4) ——— and BEERS, A. H.
    1943. THE BOLETACEAE OF NORTH CAROLINA. 96 pp., illus. Chapel Hill, N. C. (Dover reprint.)
(5) ——— and COUCH, J. N.
    1928. THE GASTEROMYCETES OF THE EASTERN UNITED STATES AND CANADA. 201 pp., illus. Chapel Hill, N. C. (Dover reprint.)
(6) GRAHAM, V. O.
    1944. MUSHROOMS OF THE GREAT LAKES REGION. Chicago Acad. Sci. Spec. Pub. 5, 390 pp., illus. (Dover reprint.)
(7) GÜSSOW, H. T., and ODELL, W. S.
    1927. MUSHROOMS AND TOADSTOOLS . . . 274 pp., illus. Ottawa.
(8) HARD, M. E.
    1908. THE MUSHROOM, EDIBLE AND OTHERWISE: ITS HABITAT AND ITS TIME OF GROWTH. 609 pp., illus. Columbus, Ohio.
(9) KAUFFMAN, C. H.
    1918. THE AGARICACEAE OF MICHIGAN. Mich. Geol. and Biol. Survey Pub. 26, Biol. Ser. 5, 923 pp., illus. [2 v.] (Dover reprint.)
(10) KRIEGER, L. C. C.
    1920. COMMON MUSHROOMS OF THE UNITED STATES. Natl. Geog. Mag. 37: [387]–439, illus.
(11) ———
    1935. A POPULAR GUIDE TO THE HIGHER FUNGI (MUSHROOMS) OF NEW YORK STATE. N. Y. State Mus. Handb. 11, 538 pp., illus.
(12) MCILVAINE, C., and MACADAM, R. K. (Dover reprint.)
    1912. TOADSTOOLS, MUSHROOMS, FUNGI, EDIBLE AND POISONOUS: ONE THOUSAND AMERICAN FUNGI. 749 pp., illus. Indianapolis, Ind.
(13) MARSHALL, N. L.
    1901. THE MUSHROOM BOOK . . . 167 pp., illus. New York.
(14) MURRILL, W. A.
    1916. EDIBLE AND POISONOUS MUSHROOMS . . . 76 pp., illus. New York.
(15) PATTERSON, F. W., and CHARLES, V. K.
    1915. MUSHROOMS AND OTHER COMMON FUNGI. U. S. Dept. Agr. Dept. Bul. 175, 64 pp., illus.
(16) THOMAS, W. S.
    1928. FIELD BOOK OF COMMON GILLED MUSHROOMS . . . 332 pp., illus. New York and London.
(17) UNDERWOOD, L. M.
    1899. MOULDS, MILDEWS, AND MUSHROOMS . . . 236 pp., illus. New York.
(18) WHITE, E. A.
    1905. A PRELIMINARY REPORT ON THE HYMENIALES OF CONNECTICUT. Conn. State Geol. and Nat. Hist. Survey Bul. 3, 81 pp., illus.
(19) ———
    1910. SECOND REPORT OF THE HYMENIALES OF CONNECTICUT. Conn. State Geol. and Nat. Hist. Survey Bul. 15, 70 pp., illus.

GLOSSARY

Adnate, closely attached, as gills to stipe.

Adnexed, gills reaching the stem but not adnate to it.

Anastomosing, united by running together irregularly, as of gills or veins with each other.

Annulus, the ring on the stem of a mushroom formed by the separation of the veil from the margin of the cap.

Apex, in mushrooms, the extremity of the stem nearest the gills.

Appendiculate, having an appendage hanging in small fragments.

Areolate, divided into little areas or patches.

Ascending, rising somewhat obliquely upward or curving.

Asci, plural of ascus.

Ascomycetes, group of fungi in which the spores are produced in saclike cells called asci.

Ascus, microscopic saclike cell in which spores, generally eight in number, are developed.

Attenuate, becoming gradually narrowed or smaller.

Azonate, without zones or circular bands of different color.

Basidium, an enlarged cell upon which spores are borne.

Bulbous, applied to stem of a mushroom with bulblike swelling at the base.

Campanulate, bell-shaped.

Cartilaginous, gristly, firm, and tough.

Cespitose, growing in tufts or clumps.

Coriaceous, of a leathery texture.

Corrugated, having a wrinkled appearance.

Cortex, an outer rindlike layer.

Crenate, notched at the edge, notches blunt, not sharp as in a serrated edge.

Cuticle, skinlike layer on the outer surface of cap and stem.

Deciduous, falling off at maturity.

Decurrent, applied to gills that are prolonged down the stem.

Dentate, toothed.

Dimidiate, halved.

Distant, applied to gills that are not close.

Emarginate, when gills are notched or scooped out at junction with stem.

Excentric, not central.

Exoperidium, outer layer of the peridium.

Expanded, spread out, as the pileus (cap) from convex to plane.

Fibrillose, appearing to be covered with or composed of minute fibers.

Fibrous, clothed with small fibers.

Floccose, downy, woolly.

Free, said of gills not attached to the stem.

Genus, a group of closely related species.

Gibbous, swollen at one side.

Glabrous, smooth.

Gleba, spore-bearing tissue in Gastromycetes.

Granular, covered with or composed of granules.

Gregarious, growing together in numbers in the same locality.

Habitat, natural place of growth of a plant.

Hygrophanous, watery when moist, opaque when dry.

Hymenium, the fruit-bearing surface.

Hymenophore, the sporophore or fruiting body.

Imbricate, overlapping like shingles.

Infundibuliform, funnel-shaped.

Innate, adhering by growth.

Involute, rolled inward.

Lanceolate, tapering to both ends.

Line, one-twelfth of an inch.

Marginate, having a well-defined border.

Obovate, broad end upward or toward the apex.

Partial, said of a veil clothing the stem and reaching to the edge of the cap but not extending beyond it.

Pellicle, a thin skin.

Pileate, having a cap or pileus.

Pileus, cap of a fungus.

Plane (of pileus), with a flat surface.

Plicate, folded like a fan.

Pruinose. covered with a bloom or powder.

Reflexed, turned back.

Resupinate, attached to the matrix by the back, the hymenium facing outward.

Reticulate, marked with cross lines like the meshes of a net.

Revolute, rolled backward or upward.

Ring, annulus, a part of the veil adhering in the form of a ring to the stem of an agaric.

Rugose, wrinkled.

Serrate, saw-toothed.

Sinuate, wavy, as the margin of gills.

Species, the smallest group of plants or animals to which distinctive and invariable characters can be assigned.

Stipe, stem of a mushroom.

Striate, marked with parallel or radiating lines.

Stuffed, said of a stem filled with material of a different texture from its walls.

Sulcate, grooved, marked with furrows.

Tomentose, densely pubescent with matted wool.

Tubercle, wartlike excrescence.

Umbilicate, with a central depression.

Umbo, central elevation.

Undulate, wavy.

Universal, said of the veil or volva which entirely envelopes the fungus when young.

Ventricose, swollen in the middle.

Villose, covered with long, weak hairs.

Viscid, moist and sticky.

Viscous, gluey.

Zonate, marked with concentric bands of color.

INDEX OF SPECIES

Descriptions of the species will be found on the pages indicated.

	Page
Agaricus arvensis	36
campestris	36
placomyces	37
rodmani	37
silvicola	36
subrufescens	37
Amanita caesarea	8
muscaria	7
phalloides	6
strobiliformis	8
Amanitopsis vaginata	9
Armillaria mellea	14
ventricosa	15
Boletus bicolor	47
chrysenteron	47
edulis	47
felleus	45
granulatus	45
luteus	45
Calvatia cyathiformis	55
gigantea	55
Cantharellus aurantiacus	18
cibarius	17
Claudopus nidulans	31
Clitocybe dealbata	20
illudens	20
monadelpha	18
multiceps	19
ochropurpurea	19
Collybia radicata	23
velutipes	23
Coprinus atramentarius	41
comatus	40
micaceus	41

	Page
Cortinarius cinnamomeus	34
lilacinus	34
Daedalea quercina	50
Fistulina hepatica	44
Fomes applanatus	48
lucidus	48
Galera tenera	35
Geaster hygrometricus	56
Hydnum coralloides	51
erinaceus	51
Hygrophorus chrysodon	28
coccineus	28
conicus	28
hypothejus	28
Hypholoma appendiculatum	39
perplexum	40
sublateritium	39
Ithyphallus impudicus	52
Lactarius deliciosus	26
indigo	26
Lentinus lecomtei	30
lepideus	30
Lepiota americana	13
morgani	10
naucina	12
procera	10
Lycoperdon pyriforme	54
Marasmius oreades	29
rotula	29
Merulius lacrymans	50
Morchella esculenta	57
Mutinus caninus	53
Mycena galericulata	25
Naucoria semiorbicularis	35

	Page
Omphalia campanella	21
Panaeolus retirugis	43
Panus stypticus	31
Pholiota adiposa	33
caperata	33
marginata	33
squarrosa	33
Pleurotus ostreatus	16
sapidus	16
Pluteus cervinus	32
Polyporus betulinus	49
frondosus	49
sulphureus	49
Polystictus cinnabarinus	50
pergamenus	50
versicolor	50
Psathyrella disseminata	42
Russula emetica	27
virescens	27
Strobilomyces strobilaceus	48
Stropharia semiglobata	38
Tricholoma equestre	22
nudum	22
personatum	22
russula	23
terreum	22
Volvaria bombycina	31